PORTUGUESE PALISSY WARE

.

PORTUGUESE PALISSY WARE

A Survey of Ceramics from Caldas da Rainha, 1853–1920

MARSHALL P. KATZ

Hudson Hills Press · New York

First Edition

© 1999 by Marshall P. Katz

Published in the United States by
Hudson Hills Press, Inc., 122 East 25th Street, 5th Floor, New York, NY 10010-2936.

Distributed in the United States, its territories and possessions, and Canada by National Book Network.
Distributed in the United Kingdom, Eire, and Europe by Art Books International Ltd.

Editor and Publisher: Paul Anbinder

Copy Editor: Virginia Wageman

Proofreader: Lydia Edwards

Indexer: Karla J. Knight

Designer: Howard I. Gralla

Composition: Angela Taormina

Manufactured in Japan by Dai Nippon Printing Company.

Library of Congress Cataloguing-in-Publication Data

Katz, Marshall P.
Portuguese Palissy ware : a survey of ceramics from Caldas da Rainha, 1853–1920 /
Marshall P. Katz. — 1st ed.
p.   cm.
Includes bibliographical references and index.
ISBN 0-933920-63-6 (cloth : alk paper)
1. Pottery, Portuguese — Portugal — Caldas da Rainha.   2. Palissy, Bernard,
1510?–1590 — Influence.   I. Title.
NK4126.C3K38   1999
738.3'09469'42 — dc21.   98-40056
                                                                      CIP

Endpaper: Tiles with top border tiles, attributed to Rafael Bordalo Pinheiro, ca. 1890 (see no. 141)

Contents

Acknowledgments

Thanks to the Portuguese embassy, I was introduced to CENCAL (Centro de Formação Profissional Para a Indústria Cerâmica), a vocational training center in Caldas da Rainha for ceramics. Here I met Eduarda Fernandes, a staff member, who helped organize my research efforts in Portugal and provided all the necessary translations. Without her dedication, perseverance, and belief in this project, this book would not have been possible. Eduarda, you have my heartfelt thanks. Special thanks are due as well to Dr. António Maria de Sousa, director of the Museu de Cerâmica in Caldas da Rainha, for new photographs from the museum's comprehensive collection, many examples of which have not previously been published. Thanks also go to staff member Cristina Horta for valuable information on the marks of Rafael Bordalo Pinheiro, and to Joaquim José Alves Saloio, a local Pinheiro collector, for information on nineteenth-century Caldas ceramics in general and on Rafael and Gustavo Pinheiro in particular.

Special gratitude goes to Manuel Gandra, a historical researcher who provided the most recent and (to date) unpublished findings on the life of Manuel Cipriano Gomes Mafra. António José Neto, director of CENCAL, graciously permitted me to use its facilities and avail myself of its excellent ceramics library. Rafael Salinas Calado's writings and research on the ceramics history of Caldas da Rainha made my task much easier.

I am especially indebted to João B. Serra, author and research specialist, University of Lisbon, for conducting additional studies into the history and lives of the Caldas ceramists. Ana Cristina Leite, director of the Museu da Cidade and the Museu Rafael Bordalo Pinheiro, Lisbon, and staff member Helena Lopes both provided valuable information on the life of Pinheiro as well as photographs for many of Pinheiro's finest works. Further thanks go to Maria Eduarda Leal Coelho, Museu da Fundação Ricardo do Espírito Santo Silva, Lisbon, for photographs from that museum's superb collection.

I also wish to thank three special antique dealers — Charles Murphy, Animal Art Antiques, New Orleans; Rita and Ian Smythe, Britannia Limited, London; and Connie and Dick Aranosian, Cara Antiques, Newtown, Pennsylvania — for the many photographs they provided. Collectors Marty Frenkel and Barbara Barbara of Los Angeles, Moe and Toni Wizenberg of Oklahoma City, and David Kozloff and Alex Speyer III of Pittsburgh supplied photographs from their collections. Kátia and Frederick Elsea of Los Angeles provided valuable historical information and generously proofread Portuguese text in the manuscript. Many others helped along the way: Sarah Nichols, chief curator and curator of decorative arts, Carnegie Museum of Art, Pittsburgh; Robert Lehr, Paris; Joshua Green, director of ceramics, Manchester Craftsmen's Guild, Pittsburgh; and Dr. Henry Gailliot, Pittsburgh. This book has been greatly improved by Kate Maloy and Virginia Wageman, who edited the manuscript and made many insightful suggestions. Marge Hasson, my secretary, patiently worked with me, kindling my enthusiasm and easing my frustrations.

My deepest gratitude goes to my publisher, Paul Anbinder, for believing in this book and supporting my efforts. And lastly, I am forever grateful to my lifelong partner, best friend, and wife, Wallis, who accompanied me to Portugal, London, Los Angeles, and New Orleans and walked through countless museums and bookstores, all with total encouragement and good cheer.

Introduction

My interest in Portuguese Palissy ware began with research for an earlier book on French Palissy ware,[1] when my curiosity about the French ceramists' Iberian neighbors led me to the town of Caldas da Rainha, Portugal. The works of Portuguese ceramists are generally unknown beyond the western shores of the Iberian Peninsula, despite a centuries-old ceramics industry, still flourishing today, whose origins can be traced to the Roman occupation. Of particular interest is a group of second-half-of-the-nineteenth-century potters from Caldas da Rainha, sixty-five miles north of Lisbon, whose works were strongly influenced by the sixteenth-century French potter Bernard Palissy. We will survey the period that begins with the work of Manuel Cipriano Gomes Mafra in 1853 and ends with the death of Manuel Gustavo Bordalo Pinheiro in 1920.

For these sixty-seven years, at least twenty-five factories in Caldas da Rainha produced a variety of ceramic ware.[2] Many of these ceramics were in the Palissy rustic tradition, depicting in natural colors small animals, reptiles, fish, shells, flora, and fauna. They were exported throughout the world, principally to England, Brazil, and the United States. The Palissy-revival era in Portugal followed ten years after a corresponding period began in France. It is doubtful there was any direct correlation between the two, for there is no evidence that any of the French and Portuguese ceramists ever knew one another or visited each other's countries, nor is there any written or oral record to suggest any form of cooperation or technology transfer between French and Portuguese ceramists. Likewise, there is no indication that French ceramist Charles-Jean Avisseau's 1843 rediscovery of Bernard Palissy's sixteenth-century ceramics secrets of lead oxide fusion and enameling had a direct relationship to the development of majolica in Portugal. Avisseau's accomplishments may have indirectly contributed to the development of majolica in England,[3] but by the late 1840s and 1850s lead-based glazes were used in several countries.

The renewal of interest in Palissy ware, mainly in Europe, during the mid–nineteenth century was principally the result of two phenomena that took place just over a year apart. The first was Avisseau's 1843 discovery and refinement of Bernard Palissy's ceramics secrets. The second was the republication of Palissy's writings in 1844, after a gap of nearly seventy years. At the same time a renewed interest in Renaissance art forms was widespread.

By 1853, when Portuguese ceramist Manuel Cipriano Gomes (later known as Manuel Mafra) first established a Palissy ware factory in Caldas da Rainha, French Palissyists were already winning awards in international exhibitions, including the 1851 Great International Exhibition at the Crystal Palace in London. During the next thirty years, the Caldas ceramics industry, steeped in the Bernard Palissy tradition and spearheaded by Mafra, grew rapidly and spawned a group of talented artists to energize their growing enterprises. This feverish activity spiked in 1884, when Rafael Bordalo Pinheiro established the Fábrica de Faianças das Caldas da Rainha (Faience Factory of Caldas da Rainha), greatly expanding the Caldas ceramics repertoire. Despite a cornucopia of commercial, industrial, and residential products, Pinheiro maintained the Palissy tradition by designing and producing ceramic rustic ware, some pieces of which rival many works

9

from France. Yet, surprisingly, the Palissy revival did not spread to any other ceramics centers in Portugal; it remained exclusive to Caldas.

Pinheiro trained nearly all the best Caldas ceramists in the next generation. He is the most thoroughly researched of the Portuguese Palissyists, with the Rafael Bordalo Pinheiro Museum in Lisbon dedicated exclusively to his life and works. Today the Pinheiro factory in Caldas (though not in its original location) continues to produce decorative tableware, most of which is exported to the United States. It also maintains and displays a comprehensive collection of Pinheiro's original molds and casts.

This book not only focuses on the two major proponents of the Portuguese Palissy revival, Mafra and Pinheiro, but also surveys the works of other important ceramists, including José Alves Cunha, José Francisco de Sousa, and Manuel Gustavo Bordalo Pinheiro.

Today works of these artists are found in virtually every Portuguese museum concerned with the decorative arts, and they grace the collections of enthusiastic Portuguese connoisseurs. Examples are also conserved in museums and private collections in other countries around the world.

This book provides the most extensive survey to date of the Palissy-inspired Caldas ceramists in a single publication. For some readers, it will serve as an introduction to this fascinating era in ceramics history. For others, more acquainted with the subject, it will present and celebrate in a single resource the works and achievements of all the notable Portuguese Palissyists.

Reference is made throughout the text to *faience*, the literal translation for the Portuguese word *faiança*. While faience (see Glossary) has a very specific ceramics definition, its meaning in many countries, especially Portugal, includes *majolica* and *Palissy ware*. It is to this latter usage that we refer. The term *majolica* also has multiple meanings. For our purposes we use the British definition, lead-glazed earthenware, more fully described in the Glossary.

Bernard Palissy

Surrounded by controversy both during his life and since, Bernard Palissy has been the subject of numerous writings, including his own. During the past two hundred years, historians have questioned his legendary accomplishments in a variety of scientific fields, but there is little doubt that his discoveries in lead-based ceramics alone would have propelled him to the height of his profession and assured his prominence in decorative arts history. Interest in Palissy peaked during the nineteenth-century Victorian era, then waned until the mid-1980s, when his Parisian workshop was uncovered during excavations of the Louvre. Interest surged again in 1990 upon the four-hundredth anniversary of his death. As recently as 1996, certain ceramic fragments found in Palissy's Parisian workshop sparked theories that he might have created the mysterious Saint-Porchaire ceramics (see Glossary), of which fewer than one hundred pieces are known.

The most recent publication on the life of Bernard Palissy — artisan to kings, writer, savant, philosopher, lecturer, naturalist, religionist, scientist, and discoverer — suggests that he was born in 1510 in the small town of Agen, approximately eighty-five miles southeast of Bordeaux, France.[4] Palissy's parentage and early years are obscure. His father was probably an artisan because Palissy was able to draw and paint, skills that were often passed from father to son. A talented student, Palissy learned the arts of portraiture and stained-glass painting as well as cartography and possibly glassmaking.

In his late teens, perhaps around 1528, Palissy left Agen to travel, primarily in southwestern France, where he earned his living by means of the trades he had learned in Agen.[5] He no doubt moved from one town to another, seeking employment as a portrait painter, stained-glass artist, or land surveyor, and remaining in each town until he ran out of work or earned enough money to continue his journeys. It is likely that during his years of travel Palissy pursued interests in naturalism, alchemy, geothermy, and underground springs and wells, all of which became subjects of his later writings.

In the latter 1530s Palissy settled in Saintes, a small town in southwestern France about sixty-five miles north of Bordeaux. There he married and raised a family of six children. Around 1539 or 1540 an event occurred that changed Palissy's life. Years later, in his book, *L'art de terre*, he wrote:

> There was shown to me an earthen cup, turned and enameled with so much beauty, that from time to time I entered into controversy with my own thoughts, recalling to mind several suggestions that some people had made to me in fun, when I was painting portraits. Then, seeing that these were falling out of request in the country where I dwelt, and that glass-painting was also little patronized, I began to think that if I should discover how to make enamels, I could make earthen vessels and other things very prettily, because God had gifted me with some knowledge of drawing.[6]

During the next decade (1540–50), Palissy and his family would experience ridicule and the brink of starvation as the impoverished potter, with no prior knowledge of ceramics, searched fervently for the secret of enamels. Unable to seek advice from others, Palissy hand ground all manner of chemical substances and fired these on fragments of earthenware pottery in his crude oven, with no knowledge of proper temperatures and firing times. After nearly five years of trial and error, he was able to produce a smooth white enamel, the basis for his other colors. For the balance of the decade, however, he continued to encounter numerous obstacles and to incur tremendous expenses. Many trials were spoiled because of overheating, others due to underheating; some were baked in the front, but not in the back; many colors burned before others melted; pieces exploded, ruining entire batches.

Finally, he was able to make some pieces that he could sell, but it was never easy:

> At last I found means to make several vessels of different enamels intermixed in the manner of jasper. That fed me for several years. . . . When I had discovered how to make my rustic pieces, I was in greater trouble and vexation than before; for having made a certain number of rustic basins, and having put them to bake, my enamels turned out some beautiful and well melted, others ill melted; others were burnt, because they were composed of different materials, that were fusible in different degrees — the green of the lizards was burnt before the color of the serpents was melted; and the color of the serpents, lobsters, tortoises, and crabs was melted before the white had attained any beauty. All these defects caused me such labor and heaviness of spirit, that before I could render my enamels fusible at the same degree of heat, I thought I should be at the door of my sepulcher.[7]

Throughout this ordeal Palissy often ran out of money and turned to glass and portrait painting as well as land surveying to support his family. The potter's finances were so precarious he even burned his floorboards and furniture to fuel the oven. He and his family were spurned by neighbors, who thought him to be crazy.

By about 1550, after nearly ten years of frustration, disappointment, and scorn, Palissy at last achieved enough success to support his family modestly. But it would be during the next several years that Palissy developed his *figulines rustiques*, or rustic ware–style of ceramics (the representation of pond life in naturalistic settings), for which he became renowned. One can imagine the young Palissy wandering the forests and streams of southwestern France making sketches of the animal life that would become the theme for his later works. To render each piece as realistically as possible, Palissy turned to molding his subjects: snakes, lizards, frogs, shells, fish, insects, leaves, and ferns. He worked in high relief, often hollowing the backs of his plates. His glistening enamels and colorful glazes soon attracted wealthy and powerful patrons, including the high constable Anne de Montmorency, the most powerful man in France next to the king.

The Protestant Reformation, meanwhile, had reached Saintes, where Palissy became an ardent reformer and is said to have even conducted secret scripture readings and prayer services on Sunday mornings. The practice of Protestantism in France was banned by various kings throughout the sixteenth century. Practitioners, along with innocent bystanders, were slaughtered, imprisoned, and tortured for heresy, although the magistrates and administrators empowered to oversee the law were not always passionate in carrying out the orders of the throne. To a certain extent this was true in Saintes, although Palissy's closest religious mentor was executed there in 1557 as a heretic. In fact, Palissy, along with several others, was the subject of an arrest warrant the following year, but there is no evidence in Palissy's case that the warrant was executed. Despite decades of scourges and painful retribution, it is estimated that nearly 25 percent of the population in France had turned to Protestantism by the close of the sixteenth century.[8]

1 Plate, workshop of
Bernard Palissy; unmarked;
ca. 1565–70. Musée National
de Céramique, Sèvres, France.

In late 1562 the town of Saintes was pillaged by Catholic troops. Many reformers were killed, and others went into hiding. Though Palissy sequestered himself at home, his workshop, which is believed to have been financed largely by Montmorency, was ravaged by a frenzied mob. All of the pottery that had been commissioned was destroyed. Despite the protection of his powerful patrons, Palissy was arrested for destroying sacred church images; he was taken forcibly from his home and spirited off to a Bordeaux prison to await the scaffold.

Only the intercession of Charles IX could save Palissy from hanging. Montmorency, hearing of the potter's imprisonment, interceded in his behalf with Catherine de Médicis, the queen mother and a great patron of the arts. She arranged for an edict appointing Palissy Potter and Inventor of Rustic Ware to the King (Ouvrier de Terre et Inventeur des Figulines Rustiques). The Bordeaux parliament (the local high court) freed Palissy, who returned to Saintes to learn of friends who had been slaughtered in the streets or sent to die on the gallows.

A few years later, in 1565, Catherine de Médicis and her young son, King Charles IX, probably visited Palissy in his restored workshop during a nearly two-year tour of France. It was then that Catherine is presumed to have commissioned Palissy to design and con-

2 *Plate, school of Bernard Palissy; unmarked; late sixteenth century. Musée Gustave Moreau, Paris (inv. no. 15536).*

struct a large garden grotto for her Palace of the Tuileries, which was being built in Paris near the Louvre, on the grounds of a tile works (*tuileries*) purchased by François I in 1518. Palissy moved his family to Paris that same year. He established a workshop there but was unable to complete the grotto installation because the palace project was abandoned in 1572.

Nevertheless, Palissy's efforts on the uncompleted Tuileries grotto have yielded fragments that can reasonably be assumed to be his own work.[9] This is all the more important because, sadly, there is no known rustic ware that bears the great potter's mark. Many pieces are attributed to Palissy's hand or workshop, but none can be proven conclusively to be the work of the master himself.

After religious civil wars between Catholics and Protestants culminated in the Saint Bartholomew's Day Massacre in 1572,[10] Palissy, fearing for his life, left one of his sons, Mathurin, to manage the Parisian workshop and moved the rest of his family to Sedan,[11] where he established a second atelier. There Palissy continued to receive orders for ceramics and devoted much time to exploring and refining his views on natural history. Encouraged by the Peace of La Rochelle in 1573,[12] and in order to benefit from a wide range of opinion, he traveled to Paris and invited other scholars, philosophers, scientists, and physicians to meet in free discussion. In due course, Palissy held the first open lec-

tures on natural history ever delivered in Paris. Around 1576 or 1577 Palissy returned there to live.

In 1584 Henri III became king, the third and last of the sons of Catherine de Médicis to succeed to the throne. By then France was embroiled in another religious civil war. The following year, in an effort to end the protracted religious conflict, the king made the practice of Protestantism punishable by death and imprisoned those who had previously followed that faith. In 1586 Palissy himself was again jailed briefly, and two years later, when he was about seventy-eight years old, he was incarcerated in the Bastille. Some historians believe the king met with Palissy in the prison and, in honor of his forty-five years of service to the royal family, offered to free him if he would revert to Catholicism.[13] Palissy refused. In 1589 Catherine de Médicis died and Henri III was assassinated; in 1590 Bernard Palissy died in the Bastille of malnourishment and vermin-borne disease.

3 *Plate, school of Bernard Palissy; unmarked; late six-teenth century. Musée Adrien Dubouché, Limoges, France.*

Louis-Ernest Barrias (1841–1905), Bernard Palissy, bronze. Courtyard of the Musée National de Céramique, Sèvres, France.

Chronology of Bernard Palissy (1510–1590)

1510	Bernard Palissy is born in Agen, France.
ca. 1528	Palissy begins his travels in southwestern France.
ca. 1535–40	Palissy settles in Saintes, France. He marries and subsequently has six children.
ca. 1540	Palissy begins his quest for the secret of enameling.
ca. 1550	Palissy meets with moderate success as a ceramist.
ca. 1555	Palissy begins making rustic ware and is patronized by Anne de Montmorency, high constable to the king of France.
1562	Palissy is arrested for his religious activities as a Protestant and is sentenced to hang in Bordeaux. At the urgings of Anne de Montmorency, the queen mother, Catherine de Médicis, intervenes and Palissy is appointed Potter and Inventor of Rustic Ware to King Charles IX.
1565	Catherine de Médicis and her son King Charles IX visit Saintes. Palissy is commissioned by Catherine to design and build a grotto for the Palace of the Tuileries. He moves with his family to Paris.
1567	Palissy's grotto is partially installed in the Tuileries. Anne de Montmorency, Palissy's supporter among the royalty, is killed in battle.
1572	Protestants are slain in the Saint Bartholomew's Day Massacre. Palissy moves to Sedan, France.
1573	The Peace of La Rochelle is declared and Palissy is able to visit Paris.
ca. 1576	Palissy returns to Paris to live.
1588	Palissy is imprisoned in the Bastille for his religious beliefs.
1590	Bernard Palissy dies while in prison.

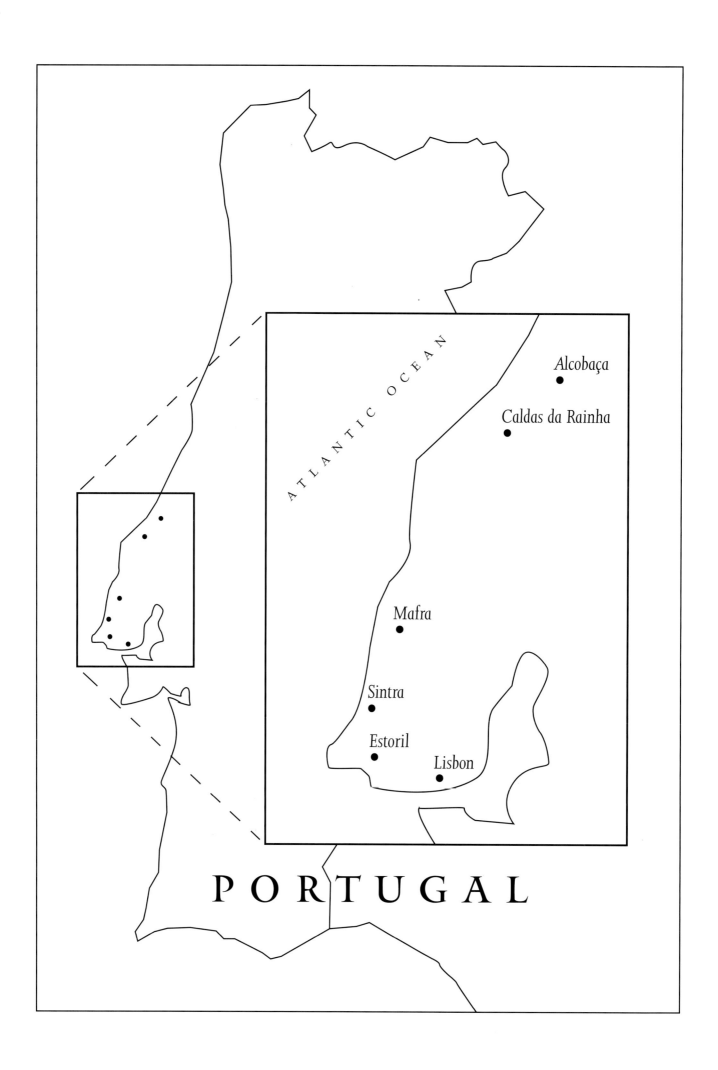

ATLANTIC OCEAN

Alcobaça

Caldas da Rainha

Mafra

Sintra

Estoril

Lisbon

P O R T U G A L

Portuguese Ceramics

Ceramic ware was first made in what is now Portugal by the Romans who occupied the Iberian Peninsula from about 200 B.C. to A.D. 300. The oldest written mention of this work dates to the thirteenth century in the form of order receipts from the town of Coimbra.[14] Although earthenware pottery, with or without decoration, has probably been produced continuously since Roman times, faience ceramic ware (*faiança* in Portuguese), as it was perfected by Bernard Palissy in the sixteenth century, was made by Portuguese followers of Palissy in the second half of the nineteenth century. These products are also called majolica, a word coined by the Minton factory in England around 1851.

The year in which faience production began in Portugal is not known, nor do any examples of early pieces remain. "Lisbon porcelain" is mentioned in historical documents from 1563 and 1582[15] (the term "porcelain" having been used in Portugal to refer at first to Chinese export porcelain and later to domestic porcelain and faience).

Accounts from 1619, 1620, and 1625 describe a thriving porcelain industry in Lisbon.[16] Archaeological discoveries in Europe, Brazil, and Africa have uncovered numerous examples of seventeenth-century Portuguese faience, suggesting a far-reaching export trade. More than six hundred pieces found just since 1981 in Holland date from the first half of the seventeenth century. But the Portuguese trade in faience dwindled later in that century as other production centers grew up in Holland — in Amsterdam, Antwerp, Haarlem, Rotterdam, and especially Delft — and in Italy, Spain, and Germany.

At about the same time, and into the eighteenth century, Portuguese faience generally became heavier, the enamel coarser, and the painting indifferent. Works from noted faience centers in Alcobaça and Mafra deteriorated until the mid–eighteenth century, despite the facts that Portugal was the wealthiest nation in Europe under King João V (r. 1706–1750) and that its art and culture flourished during this time.[17]

Only two ceramics centers maintained high standards in these years: Monte Sinai in Lisbon and the faience factories in Coimbra. The Lisbon makers' line of unique pottery, decorated in blue with well-painted figures of birds and animals, was very successful. Coimbra ceramic ware was expressive and informal, often glazed with a thick blue palette containing baroque elements in original interpretations.

In the wake of the Lisbon earthquake of 1755, the most devastating European natural disaster of that century, the Marquis de Pombal, minister to King Joseph I (r. 1750–1777), prohibited the importation of all foreign pottery except from India and China. In 1767, under the direction of Italian ceramist Tommaso Brunetto, Pombal established the Real Fábrica de Cerâmica (Royal Ceramics Factory) in Lisbon, which offered training in the latest technical and production methods in order to seed other local and national ceramics centers. Production geared to fashionable tastes generated such innovative designs as animal-shaped tureens, bowls with fish, and the famous cabbage-leaf plates that would be adapted one hundred years later into popular tea services by Caldas ceramists Manuel Mafra (no. 26) and José Alves Cunha (no. 68). From 1769 to 1796, through successive managements, the Royal Factory spawned a bevy of Lisbon potteries, including the well-known Real Fábrica da Bica do Sapato. In Coimbra, the talented ceramist Manuel da Costa Brioso developed lovely, strong-colored molded pieces in which landscapes, arabesques,[18] and bouquets contrasted with hand-stippled and marbled finishes. Their appeal was so immediate that they soon dominated popular faience.

In 1784 Domingos Vandelli, an Italian doctor and botanist who emigrated to Portugal to become a teacher at the University of Coimbra, created a new type of Coimbra faience (actually, it was a type of stoneware) that became known as *louça de vandel* (vandel china). This work is characterized by balanced colors, predominately yellows and greens. Throughout the late 1700s many other successful faience factories were established in Aveiro, Oporto, Gaia, Viana do Castelo, and Estremoz.

The Real Fábrica do Cavaquinho (Royal Factory of Cavaquinho), established in Gaia in 1768, produced magnificent works characterized by transparent enamel, fineness of painting, and delicate molding. This important ceramics factory operated until 1860, though it closed between 1808 and 1815 during the French invasions. Its important ceramists and owners were Bento Fernandes de San Francisco, João Bernado Guedes, João Raimundo Noguera, Manuel José Soares, João da Rocha, and João José Gomes.

In 1775 the Fábrica de Miragaia was founded by João da Rocha, and it operated under the administration of the Rocha Soares family until 1852. In 1785 another factory was founded by Genoa native Jerónirmo Rossi in Santo António de Vale de Piedade. Remarkably, it sustained production under various ownerships until 1930. Its works, usually on a bluish white or lead-white background, often featured popular figures of their time, both fictional and real.

The Portuguese ceramics factories that arose by the end of the eighteenth century went on to evolve, consolidate, and flourish, making nineteenth-century ceramics the richest in the country's history. Fashionable designs that incorporated reigning international tastes reflected neoclassical, romantic, and art nouveau movements. Dom Fernando II, husband of Queen Maria II (r. 1826–1853), was passionately interested in ceramics, not simply as a collector, but as a practitioner and a mentor to other ceramists.[19] He took Prague-born Wenceslau Cifka, a forestry engineer turned artist, under his wing, and eventually this talented and versatile artist introduced photography to Portugal and helped acquire ceramics for the royal collection. During Cifka's illustrious ceramics career at the Fábrica Constância in Lisbon, which lasted until his death in 1883, he produced masterful imitations of Urbino maiolica and elaborate *grottesco* compositions.[20]

During the nineteenth century many successful ceramics factories and workshops were established throughout Portugal, despite civil war and widespread social unrest. Among them was the factory of Carvalhino in Oporto,[21] founded in 1840 by Tomás Nunes da Cunha and António Monteiro Cantarino. It was enlarged in 1853, underwent numerous changes of name and ownership, and continued well into the twentieth century.

In 1849 the widow Lamego founded a ceramics factory in Lisbon. It produced red porcelain until 1863, when it turned to faience. By 1898 the factory employed nearly one hundred people and had expanded its products to include ornate ceramic ware and hand-painted tiles, which it produces to this day.

The ceramics factory of Sacavém was established in 1850 by glassmaker Manuel Joaquim Afonso to produce decorated and undecorated tableware. The factory was later sold to British interests, which expanded and upgraded the product line. Between 1878 and 1884, Fernando II decorated and fired his own works in the facility. As a result, the company became known for a short time as the Real Fábrica da Sacavém. In the twentieth century it underwent additional ownership changes and ultimately became known as Gilman & Gilbert.

The ceramics factory of Devezas was founded in Gaia in 1865 by António Alveida da Costa. By 1890 it employed seven hundred people. Its success was in large measure due to its school of drawing and modeling, which graduated hundreds of skilled workers. The director of the school, Teixeira Lopes, was himself a well-known sculptor whose works are in several Portuguese museums. The company still exists as Fábrica do Costa.

The factory of Manuel Ferreira da Bernarda, in Alcobaça, known as Fábrica da Louça, was founded by José dos Reis in 1875. Its product line, sold locally, consisted of inexpensive hand-painted and printed ware made from native white clay. Upon dos Reis's death in 1897, the factory was leased to Manuel Ferreira da Bernarda, Jr., whose descendants still operate the factory.

The great variety of nineteenth-century Portuguese ceramics factories, many of them still in operation, reflects the vast transformation of this industry during a period of social and financial instability. Their history remains a testament not only to Portuguese ceramists, but to the character of the Portuguese people.

Caldas da Rainha and Its Ceramics

The town of Caldas da Rainha, originally called Caldas de Óbidos,[22] dates to the fifteenth-century discovery of a thermal sulfurous spring with healing powers that drew visitors from near and far, including Queen Leonor de Lencastre (wife of King João II, r. 1481–1495). The story goes that the queen, who suffered from skin disease, one day passed through the region and noticed some men bathing in the sulfur-laden waters. After trying the spring herself and being immediately cured, she became determined that all her fellow citizens should have access to the miracle and in 1488 established the Leonor Thermal Hospital at the site of the spring. She also founded a lodging especially for the poor, even though she had to sell her jewels to do so. In 1488 Caldas became independent of Óbidos and changed its name to Caldas da Rainha in honor of Queen Leonor, for Caldas da Rainha means Queen's Bath.[23]

While better known for its baths, Caldas da Rainha has been a ceramics center for the past 150 years, although its ceramic products may date to the Middle Ages. The region is rich in clay pits and has always had access to dark red clay coming from Gaeiras and white clay from Águas Santas, both within a mile of Caldas. Historically, people in the area used these clays to make vessels and casks to store food and water. Records show that the rich clay from Caldas was used for ceramics production as early as the thirteenth century.

Two decorated red clay pitchers, now in the collection of the Museu de Artes Decorativas Portuguesas in Lisbon, are examples of fifteenth-century Caldas pottery, according to ceramics expert Joaquim de Vasconcelos.[24] Avelino Soares Belo, a respected Caldas potter who conducted research in the archives of the Leonor Thermal Hospital, discovered that in 1488 there were at least three potters in Caldas: Vicente Annes, Alvaro Annes, and Francisco Lopes.[25] The latter was a supplier of red clay earthen tableware, as evidenced by the following fifteenth-century price list from Lopes in the hospital archives:

> small bowl with handle — 5 reis
>
> pan — 3 reis
>
> large bowl to prepare dough — 40 reis
>
> large pan for cow butter — 12 reis[26]

Records indicate that in 1508 Caldas potters supplied tableware not only to the hospital, but also to the Madre de Deus Convent in Lisbon.[27] By 1522, according to other hospital records, there were at least four additional potters in Caldas, including Lopo Dias, who also supplied the hospital. By 1575 the hospital's supplier was Miguel Fernandes. Demographic data show that potters were significant to the urban structure of Caldas da Rainha in the sixteenth and seventeenth centuries. Seventeenth-century Portuguese historian Jorge de São Paulo wrote about Caldas as an industrial ceramics center celebrated for its emerald-green glaze. However, other historical records describe seventeenth-century Caldas tableware as "thick, generally plain . . . covered with green enamel," or "colored blue and honey."[28]

During the eighteenth century, with ceramics still important to the Caldas economy, potters were classified as red clay potters or glaze potters. They produced a variety of

common tableware, as described in a report by a physician, Seixas Brandão, in 1781:
"The only factories in Caldas are potteries where tableware is made, both for local use
and in other markets, and although crude, are good enough to use, saving visitors the
need to bring their own."[29]

There are no ceramic pieces that can be ascribed to any particular Caldas potter from
the seventeenth or eighteenth centuries. However, we can safely assume that a small pottery community existed in Caldas by the end of the sixteenth century and that these artisans produced red clay common tableware to supply the domestic market, including the
hospital. Further, there existed a simultaneous production of glazed ceramics that, at

23

least by the eighteenth century, attracted a market of more demanding buyers, including nobility and even some in the royal house — at least those who frequented the Caldas thermal hospital.

Writer and art critic Ramalho Ortigão maintained, in an 1886 text about the late-eighteenth-century Caldas ceramics production, that it had "a skill of notable imitation with an incomparable glaze giving the products a bright shine, iridescent like the shimmering sun on water, bathing the clay with a diamond mantle, translucent, ravishing, wonderful."[30] However, Caldas da Rainha suffered greatly during the political and economic crises of the first two decades of the nineteenth century. The Portuguese government converted the thermal hospital to an army field unit, thus depriving the town of this important income source. Furthermore, with the royal family moving to Brazil in 1807 under the threat of French invasion, the town lost its status as a royal destination. The area was devastated by the occupation of Napoleon's troops in that year, and its economic engine nearly came to a standstill.[31] Ceramics production declined dramatically. Though the British military in Portugal repelled the French the following year, the two countries continued warring on Portuguese soil for nearly another decade.

Caldas by this time was no longer an important ceramics center. Throughout the entire first half of the nineteenth century, the town produced no Caldas ceramists of distinction, and few pieces from those decades in Caldas bear any signature, mark, or date.

Nevertheless, a few factories produced ceramic ware after the early-nineteenth-century crises. The first of the new factories to be opened was that of Dona Maria dos Cacos (fl. 1820–1853), the best-known Caldas ceramist from this period. She claimed the title "dona" — one normally reserved for the aristocracy — until her retirement in 1853, though it was not officially bestowed. This is particularly amusing since the literal translation of her name, "Mary of the Crocks," is so plebeian that it mocks even a self-assumed aristocratic moniker.

Although records and accounts of dos Cacos's activities are sparse, it is clear that her factory was located at rua do Jogo da Bola in Caldas, where for more than thirty years she produced inexpensive, monochromatic tableware in highly glazed faience, which she sold at county fairs throughout Portugal. Her ceramics are characterized by a thick body made from clay from Oiteiros.[32] Her varied production included diminutive figurines of people and animals as well as candlesticks, bowls, and jars, which enjoyed wide popularity throughout the country and restored a degree of Caldas's waning fame.

Numerous examples of dos Cacos's work survive in Caldas museums and private collections. During *Expo Caldas '77*, a ceramics exhibition organized in 1977 by the Malhoa Museum in Caldas, no fewer than forty-two pieces attributed to dos Cacos were assembled. Yet all are merely *attributed* to Maria dos Cacos since none bears any mark or signature.

Eventually, the dos Cacos factory, the largest and most successful in early-nineteenth-century Caldas da Rainha, proved instrumental in launching the era of Portuguese Palissy ware that made Caldas a major ceramics center. As the following discussion will show, a twenty-year-old factory employee changed the course of Caldas ceramics history by adapting and promoting a style originally devised by Bernard Palissy.

The Portuguese Followers of Bernard Palissy

Between 1853 and 1920 five major ceramists founded and sparked the Portuguese Palissy movement centered exclusively in Caldas da Rainha. The movement began with Manuel Cipriano Gomes Mafra's opening of the first factory devoted to Palissy-inspired ceramics, and it ended with the death of Manuel Gustavo Bordalo Pinheiro. Scores of other ceramists included Palissy-type works in their repertoires, but none was as innovative, prolific, or skilled as Mafra, Pinheiro, José Alves Cunha, José Francisco de Sousa, and Rafael Bordalo Pinheiro, whose stories follow.

Surprisingly, the Palissy movement did not in any great measure spread to other parts of the country. Perhaps other Portuguese ceramists considered Palissy ware an exclusive specialty of Caldas da Rainha — although nothing in Portuguese literature either supports or refutes that view.

The quality of Portuguese Palissy ware, except for the works of Rafael Bordalo Pinheiro, generally does not compare favorably with that of French works from the same era in artistic rendering, color palette, or the sophistication and skill of the artists. Many pieces are colored inaccurately and contain poorly modeled, crude elements that lack crisp detail; the skin and skeletal features are not well delineated; animals display unnatural postures and expressions; and overall the works betray a naive artistic imagination. Even so, Portuguese Palissy ware possesses its own captivating charm — a style and simplicity that are attractive to connoisseurs and amateurs alike.

Manuel Cipriano Gomes Mafra (1830–1905)

In 1850 a twenty-year-old part-time waiter and potter from the nearby town of Mafra (thirty-five miles southwest of Caldas) began work at the factory of Maria dos Cacos.[33] Mafra was a small tourist town known primarily for its Manueline-style, eighteenth-century palace and basilica.[34] Manuel Cipriano Gomes, the young potter, was the grandson of Manoel and Anna Dorothea Gomes and the son of Cipriano and Izidora Maria Gomes.[35] Cipriano is believed to have been a potter. He would have learned his craft from his father (Manoel) and taught it to his son. Maria Souza, Cipriano's second wife, bore at least two daughters, Luísa and Mariana, who became important ceramics collaborators with their half-brother.

The historical record does not indicate why Manuel Cipriano Gomes moved to Caldas da Rainha, but it may be presumed that he was drawn by the growing ceramics reputation of Caldas and driven by a likely lack of economic opportunity in Mafra. By 1850 Maria dos Cacos's reputation was well established in Caldas and in some other areas of the country. Gomes probably sought employment at her factory because it was the largest in Caldas.

Historians differ with respect to Gomes's prior training. Until 1996, accounts stated that Gomes received no ceramics training in Mafra but was a waiter who learned pottery making from dos Cacos. More recent research supports the idea that he was trained as a potter by his father. That would explain why, in 1853, a scant three years after he was hired by dos Cacos, he was able to rent the entire factory from her and almost immediately become the leading local ceramics producer. He sustained that distinction for the next three decades, adopting a style totally unlike that of dos Cacos — one that required skill perhaps unparalleled in the entire country.

Gomes executed a long-term lease for the Maria dos Cacos factory in partnership with a fellow worker, António Domingos Reis, and his family. Nothing more is known of Reis, however, so he may have retired soon after the lease was signed, selling his family interest to Gomes.

Gomes, as the dominant ceramist in Caldas for the next thirty years, adopted the last name Mafra, after his birthplace. He is still known today as O Mafra (The Mafra). It is therefore likely that his earliest mark (around 1853, since none is dated) was "MCG," for Manuel Cipriano Gomes. His next mark, in the mid-1850s, was probably "MCGM" (Manuel Cipriano Gomes Mafra), which was then shortened to "MCM" (Manuel Cipriano Mafra) in the late 1850s. Soon after, Mafra changed his mark to "M. Mafra" and added an anchor, a popular symbol of the newly revived Manueline style of his hometown.

Gomes's name change is not documented, but we may conjecture that the artist, who perhaps had a flair for salesmanship, wanted to enhance his image by dropping the common Portuguese last name of Gomes in favor of one associated with arguably the most beautiful palace in Portugal and the finest example of Manueline architecture in the country.

Mafra scholars generally believe that he began working in the style of Bernard Palissy after he saw a Palissy ware plate of either sixteenth- or nineteenth-century origin that his collector friend, José Palha, purchased in Paris. Mafra might also have been influenced by the contemporary Lisbon potter Wenceslau Cifka, who is known to have made some Palissy-inspired plates — though it is more likely that Mafra influenced Cifka. Another, more speculative account suggests that Mafra was familiar with the work of both Bernard Palissy and the fifteenth-century Florentine sculptor Luca della Robbia, who specialized in glazed terra cottas, and was directly influenced by his own knowledge of both of them. It is more plausible that Mafra, like many of his French predecessors and contemporaries, was simply so captivated by the Palissy-style creations that he began making them himself, eventually devoting most of his thirty-year career to this pursuit.

Mafra's adaptations of Palissy ware differed markedly from the works of his French counterparts. In his hands, the characteristic Palissy theme — life as found in a tranquil pond — gave way to images of a fierce struggle for survival, usually between snake and lizard. This subject became so popular that it was copied by nearly every subsequent nineteenth-century Caldas ceramist and came to dominate the output of many Portuguese Palissy followers. In fact, Mafra was the first Caldas ceramist to establish an international market for his ware, principally in England and Brazil, because his style was universally appealing. Even though English ceramics factories, especially Minton, Wedgwood, and George Jones, adopted their own style of Palissy ware, England was by far Caldas's largest export customer. Today it is the best source for nineteenth-century Portuguese Palissy ware, even surpassing Portugal itself.

In addition to snakes and lizards, Mafra incorporated many other traditional Palissy elements into his works — shells, fish, frogs, crayfish, moths, beetles, caterpillars, and local flora and fauna. But unlike Palissy or his nineteenth-century French followers, Mafra incorporated a new element into his design — *musgo*, or moss. Where his French contemporaries usually arranged their naturalistic elements around rustic ponds, Mafra often placed his creatures on a bed of thick green moss, using a more-than-two-thousand-year-old Egyptian technique of pressing wet clay through a sieve. Mafra's use of moss as a principal background was as widely adopted by other Palissyists in Caldas, as were his snakes and lizards.

Mafra introduced many technical as well as subject matter innovations. He greatly enlarged the color palette to nine basic colors and shades, whereas his predecessor, Maria dos Cacos, had for thirty years produced only monochromatic works, often in green, brown, or blue. Earlier Caldas ceramics had also tended toward single-color glazes. Mafra began producing polychrome works in shades of earth tones, such as greens and browns, with accents of yellows, blues, and reds. Using lead, tin, and other metallic oxides, he achieved brilliant colors and glazes.

Mafra sometimes used cobalt oxide to produce a rich and lustrous blue, as in a large, unsigned vase with snake handles (no. 21).[36] While this work is comparable in style and quality to pieces by nineteenth-century Parisian artists, such as Victor and Achille Barbizet, or Thomas Sergent, comparing it to the signed Mafra pieces, such as two urns with snake handles (nos. 22 and 40), reveals its true lineage. It is possible, of course, that any of these French contemporaries of Mafra could have copied the vase, but the only works known to be copied by these artists were in the more formal Renaissance style, never in the rustic style.

Mafra was the first in Caldas to use a high-glaze, mottled background of browns or browns and greens (see, for example, nos. 8, 10, and 54). Many of his best-known works, such as one of the urns with snake handles (no. 22), also employ this technique. He was the first in Caldas (and perhaps in Portugal) to refine the jasper technique (see Glossary), first developed by Bernard Palissy. His glazes were especially thick and luminous, as in a plate with a central snake and smaller insects, lizards, and a frog (no. 50) and a vessel in the shape of a jug (no. 51), and in their glazes his works compare favorably to those of his contemporaries around the world. As a leader in Portuguese ceramics, an artisan of high standards, and an ambitious promoter who exhibited at ceramics fairs and major industrial and commercial exhibitions, Mafra is credited with developing an export trade in ceramics from Caldas, still an important source of the town's revenue.

Mafra's earliest employees included António Domingos Reis; his own half-sisters, Luísa and Mariana; his wife, Maria José; and António Joaquim (nicknamed Roubada). The three women refined the *verguinha* technique for making ceramic baskets (see Glossary), a common element in non-Palissian Caldas works. Until the mid-1880s, Mafra's factory remained the largest in Caldas da Rainha, employing fifteen workers at its peak.[37] Its principal markets were Portugal, Brazil, the United States, and England. The clays used were mainly white from Leiria (a town thirty miles north of Caldas) and reds from Caldas.

Mafra's renown did not escape the attention of Dom Fernando II, who both purchased and commissioned works for the royal collection, many of which can be seen today at the Paço Real (Royal Palace) and the Palácio da Pena (Pena Palace), both in Sintra. Fernando dubbed the Mafra factory "Royal Supplier to the King" and even authorized use of the crown as part of the Mafra mark. A splendid example (no. 4), one of a pair, is an urn with bird handles bearing the Portuguese royal arms and crest and impressed "M. Mafra, Caldas, Portugal" with a crown. The precise date of this privilege is not known, but it must have been relatively early in Mafra's career, perhaps in the early to mid-1860s, since the crown is used in the most common mark found on Mafra pieces today (which rarely bear dates).

Manuel Mafra had one child, a son, Eduardo Augusto, who assumed control of the factory upon his father's retirement in 1887. The new mark "M. Mafra Filho," with crown, unfortunately did not last long, for, according to Mafra, Eduardo preferred relaxing to working. After 1894 Eduardo transferred production to Augusto Baptista de Carvalho, a local ceramist, then to Pereira de Sousa, who apparently did not produce a single piece. In 1897 Manuel Mafra, who in the meantime had become active in publishing, in the progressive party, and in other community affairs, reassumed control of the factory and attempted to resuscitate it. His attempt was unsuccessful, and the factory closed that same year.

Little is known about the role Mafra played in the production process during his thirty years in charge of the factory, but given the small number of employees and Mafra's energetic nature, it is likely that he was intimately involved in all aspects of production as well as sales. He was undoubtedly the factory's artistic director as well, creating the designs of all or most of the models that were produced. Because no production records exist from this period, we cannot say precisely how many pieces the Mafra factory produced for each model. Over the factory's nearly forty years, the more popular models were no doubt made in the thousands. Unfortunately, increased demand caused problems. The number of models was greatly expanded, resulting in many designs that

4 Urn (one of a pair),
Manuel Mafra; impressed
"M. Mafra, Caldas, Portugal"
with crown; 17 in. (43 cm)
high, 13 ½ in. (34.5 cm)
diameter; ca. 1865–87.
Ricardo do Espírito Santo
Silva Foundation, Duarte Pinto
Coelho Collection, Museu de
Artes Decorativas Portuguesas,
Lisbon (inv. no. 2).

resembled one another. It is likely that Mafra resorted to mass production to satisfy
demand, diminishing the quality of his works in later years.[38]

In 1895 Manuel Mafra, with Francisco Gomes de Avelar (fl. 1875–1897), an important
ceramist in his own right, founded the Grémio dos Artistas Caldenses (Caldas Artists
Association).[39] Mafra, the founder and leading proponent of the Palissy movement in
Portugal, died on 11 November 1905, at the age of seventy-five. His legacy lives on in
both the Artists Association and in his ceramics, which are displayed in museums and
collections throughout Portugal and abroad.

29

5 Plate, Manuel Mafra; impressed "M. Mafra, Caldas, Portugal" with crown; 15½ in. (39.5 cm) diameter; ca. 1865–87. Marty Frenkel and Barbara Barbara collection, Los Angeles.

6 Plate, Manuel Mafra; impressed "M. Mafra, Caldas Rainha" with crown; 10¼ in. (26 cm) diameter; ca. 1865–87. Animal Art Antiques, New Orleans.

7 Plate, Manuel Mafra;
impressed "M. Mafra,
Caldas, Portugal" with crown;
12½ in. (32 cm) diameter;
ca. 1865–87. Marty Frenkel
and Barbara Barbara
collection, Los Angeles.

8 Plate, Manuel Mafra;
impressed "M. Mafra, Caldas,
Portugal" with crown;
15 in. (38 cm) diameter;
ca. 1865–87. Cara Antiques,
Newtown, Pennsylvania.

31

9 Plate, Manuel Mafra;
impressed "Mafra, Caldas
da Rainha" with crown;
4½ in. (11.5 cm) diameter;
ca. 1865–87. New Orleans
Museum of Art: Brooke
Hayward Duchin Collection
(acc. no. 1997.771).

10 Plate, Manuel Mafra;
impressed "M. Mafra, Caldas,
Portugal" with crown;
12 in. (30.5 cm) × 15¼ in.
(39 cm); ca. 1865–87.
Mr. and Mrs. Alexander C.
Speyer III collection,
Pittsburgh.

11 Urn with lid, attributed
to Manuel Mafra; unmarked;
31 1/8 in. (79 cm) high,
14 1/4 in. (36 cm) diameter;
ca. 1865–87. Ricardo do
Espírito Santo Silva
Foundation, Duarte Pinto
Coelho Collection, Museu de
Artes Decorativas Portuguesas,
Lisbon (inv. no. 1).

12 Plate, Manuel Mafra;
impressed "M. Mafra, Caldas,
Portugal" with crown;
9 in. (23 cm) diameter;
ca. 1865–87. New Orleans
Museum of Art: Brooke
Hayward Duchin Collection
(acc. no. 1997.770).

13 Plate, Manuel Mafra;
impressed "M. Mafra, Caldas,
Portugal" with crown;
9½ in. (24 cm) diameter;
ca. 1865–87. Marty Frenkel
and Barbara Barbara
collection, Los Angeles.

16 Plate, Manuel Mafra; impressed "M. Mafra, Caldas, Portugal" with crown; 10¼ in. (26 cm) diameter; ca. 1865–87. Britannia, Grays Antique Market, London.

17 Plate, Manuel Mafra; impressed "M. Mafra, Caldas, Portugal" with crown; 15¼ in. (38.5 cm) diameter; ca. 1865–87. New Orleans Museum of Art: Brooke Hayward Duchin Collection (acc. no. 1997.764).

18 *Plate, Manuel Mafra;
impressed "Mafra, Caldas da
Rainha" with crown and
numeral "8"; 4 in. (10 cm)
diameter; ca. 1865–87.
Animal Art Antiques,
New Orleans.*

19 *Plate, Manuel Mafra;
impressed "M. Mafra, Caldas,
Portugal" with crown;
9½ in. (24 cm) diameter;
ca. 1865–87. Animal Art
Antiques, New Orleans.*

20 *Tobacco jar, Manuel Mafra; impressed "M. Mafra, Caldas, Portugal" with anchor; 4⅜ in. (11 cm) high, 3¼ in. (8.5 cm) diameter; ca. 1865. Moe and Toni Wizenberg collection, Oklahoma City.*

21 *Urn, attributed to Manuel Mafra; unmarked; 15½ in. (39.5 cm) high, 9 in. (23 cm) diameter; ca. 1865–87. Animal Art Antiques, New Orleans.*

22 *Urn, Manuel Mafra; impressed "M. Mafra, Caldas, Portugal"; 13¼ in. (33.5 cm) high, 7⅛ in. (18 cm) diameter; ca. 1865–87. Ricardo do Espírito Santo Silva Foundation, Duarte Pinto Coelho Collection, Museu de Artes Decorativas Portuguesas, Lisbon (inv. no. 16).*

23 Plate, Manuel Mafra; impressed "Mafra, Caldas da Rainha" with crown and numeral "5"; 10 in. (25.5 cm) diameter; ca. 1865–87. New Orleans Museum of Art: Brooke Hayward Duchin Collection (acc. no. 1997.769).

24 Plate, Manuel Mafra; impressed "M. Mafra, Caldas, Portugal" with crown; 7 ½ in. (19 cm) diameter; ca. 1865–87. Marty Frenkel and Barbara Barbara collection, Los Angeles.

25 Plate, Manuel Mafra; impressed "M. Mafra, Caldas, Portugal" with anchor; 15 in. (38 cm) diameter; ca. 1865. New Orleans Museum of Art: Brooke Hayward Duchin Collection (acc. no. 1997.768).

26 Tea service, Manuel
Mafra; each piece impressed
"M. Mafra, Caldas, Portugal"
with crown; teapot 9 in.
(23 cm) high, sugar bowl
7 in. (18 cm) high, creamer
6¾ in. (17 cm) high;
ca. 1865–87. Cara Antiques,
Newtown, Pennsylvania.

27 Plate, Manuel Mafra;
impressed "MCGM" with
anchor; 4½ in. (11.5 cm)
diameter; ca. 1865.
New Orleans Museum
of Art, Brooke Hayward
Duchin Collection
(acc. no. 1997.763).

28 Plate, Manuel Mafra;
impressed "M. Mafra, Caldas,
Portugal" with crown;
4½ in. (11.5 cm) diameter;
ca. 1865–87. Animal Art
Antiques, New Orleans.

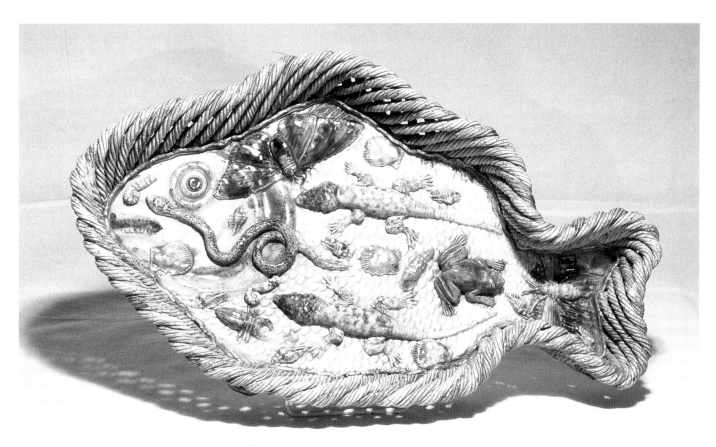

29 *Plate, Manuel Mafra;
impressed "Mafra, Caldas
da Rainha" with crown;
9 in. (23 cm) diameter;
ca. 1865–87. New Orleans
Museum of Art: Brooke
Hayward Duchin Collection
(acc. no. 1997.762).*

30 *Fish tray, attributed to
Manuel Mafra; unmarked;
11½ in. (29 cm) × 19¼ in.
(49 cm); ca. 1865–87.
Museu de Cerâmica, Caldas
da Rainha.*

33 Plate, Manuel Mafra; impressed "M. Mafra, Caldas, Portugal" with crown and incised numeral "4"; 12 in. (30.5 cm) diameter; ca. 1865–87. Cara Antiques, Newtown, Pennsylvania.

34 Plate, Manuel Mafra; impressed "M. Mafra, Caldas, Portugal" with crown and numeral "8"; 8¼ in. (21 cm) diameter; ca. 1865–87. Britannia, Grays Antique Market, London.

35 Mark and worker number on rear of plate in no. 34.

43

36 *Ewer with saucer and lid, Manuel Mafra; each piece impressed "M. Mafra, Caldas, Portugal" with crown; 11 in. (28 cm) high; ca. 1865–87. Marty Frenkel and Barbara Barbara collection, Los Angeles.*

37 *Ewer with lid and saucer, Manuel Mafra; impressed "M. Mafra, Caldas, Portugal" with crown; 11 in. (28 cm) high, 8 in. (20.5 cm) diameter; ca. 1865–87. Animal Art Antiques, New Orleans.*

38 Ewer on pedestal, Manuel
Mafra; impressed "M. Mafra,
Caldas, Portugal" with crown;
12¼ in. (31 cm) high,
7½ in. (19 cm) diameter;
ca. 1865–87. Jorge dos
Santos Alexandre collection,
Caldas da Rainha.

39 Ewer and lid with saucer,
Manuel Mafra; impressed
"M. Mafra, Caldas, Portugal"
with crown; 13¾ in. (35 cm)
high, 9½ in. (24 cm)
diameter; ca. 1865–87.
Museu de Cerâmica,
Caldas da Rainha.

40 Urn, Manuel Mafra;
impressed "M. Mafra, Caldas,
Portugal" with crown;
13¼ in. (33.5 cm) high,
9¼ in. (23.5 cm) diameter;
ca. 1865–87. Animal Art
Antiques, New Orleans.

41 Plate, Manuel Mafra; impressed "M. Mafra, Caldas, Portugal" with crown and incised numeral "6"; 16½ in. (42 cm) diameter; ca. 1865–87. Britannia, Grays Antique Market, London.

42 Plate, Manuel Mafra; impressed "M. Mafra, Caldas, Portugal" with crown; 8 in. (20.5 cm) diameter; ca. 1865–87. Animal Art Antiques, New Orleans.

45 *Plate, Manuel Mafra; impressed "M. Mafra, Caldas da Rainha" with crown and numeral "6"; 7½ in. (19 cm) diameter; ca. 1865–87. Animal Art Antiques, New Orleans.*

46 *Plate, Manuel Mafra; impressed "M. Mafra, Caldas, Portugal" with crown; 12¾ in. (32.5 cm) diameter; ca. 1865–87. Cara Antiques, Newtown, Pennsylvania.*

48

47 Plate, Manuel Mafra;
impressed "M. Mafra, Caldas,
Portugal" with crown;
15½ in. (39.5 cm) diameter;
ca. 1865–87. New Orleans
Museum of Art: Brooke
Hayward Duchin Collection
(acc. no. 1997.772).

48 Plate, Manuel Mafra;
impressed "M. Mafra, Caldas,
Portugal" with crown;
7½ in. (19 cm) diameter;
ca. 1865–87. Marty Frenkel
and Barbara Barbara
collection, Los Angeles.

49

51 *Vessel with lid and pedestal, attributed to Manuel Mafra; unmarked; 19¼ in. (49 cm) high, 11½ in. (29 cm) diameter; ca. 1865–87. Museu de Cerâmica, Caldas da Rainha.*

52 *Plate, Manuel Mafra; impressed "M. Mafra, Caldas Rainha" with crown; 7¼ in. (18.5 cm) diameter; ca. 1865–87. Animal Art Antiques, New Orleans.*

51

53 *Plate, Manuel Mafra; impressed "M. Mafra, Caldas, Portugal" with crown and numeral "4"; 12 in. (30.5 cm) diameter; ca. 1865–87. Animal Art Antiques, New Orleans.*

54 *Urn, attributed to Manuel Mafra; unmarked; 13½ in. (34.5 cm) high, 10 in. (25.5 cm) diameter; ca. 1865–87. Ricardo do Espírito Santo Silva Foundation, Duarte Pinto Coelho Collection, Museu de Artes Decorativas Portuguesas, Lisbon (inv. no. 65).*

55 Plate, Manuel Mafra; impressed "M. Mafra, Caldas, Portugal" with crown; 15½ in. (39.5 cm) diameter; ca. 1865–87. Marty Frenkel and Barbara Barbara collection, Los Angeles.

56 Plate, Manuel Mafra; impressed "M. Mafra, Caldas Rainha" with crown and numeral "6"; 10 in. (25.5 cm) diameter; ca. 1865–87. Animal Art Antiques, New Orleans.

57 Pair of urns (front and rear view), attributed to Manuel Mafra; unmarked; each 14½ in. (37 cm) high, 9¾ in. (25 cm) diameter; ca. 1865–87. Moe and Toni Wizenberg collection, Oklahoma City.

58 Pair of candlesticks,
Manuel Mafra; each
impressed "M. Mafra, Caldas,
Portugal" with crown;
each 10 in. (25.5 cm) high;
ca. 1865–87. Cara Antiques,
Newtown, Pennsylvania.

59 Plate, Manuel Mafra;
impressed "M. Mafra,
Caldas, Portugal" with crown;
4½ in. (11.5 cm) diameter;
ca. 1865–87. Animal Art
Antiques, New Orleans.

55

60 Plate, Manuel Mafra;
impressed "M. Mafra, Caldas
da Rainha" with crown and
numeral "6"; 7 in. (18 cm)
diameter; ca. 1865–87.
New Orleans Museum of
Art: Brooke Hayward
Duchin Collection
(acc. no. 1997.767).

61 Ewer, attributed to
Manuel Mafra; illegible
mark; 13 in. (33 cm) high,
8 in. (20.5 cm) diameter;
ca. 1865–87. New Orleans
Museum of Art: Brooke
Hayward Duchin Collection
(acc. no. 1997.783).

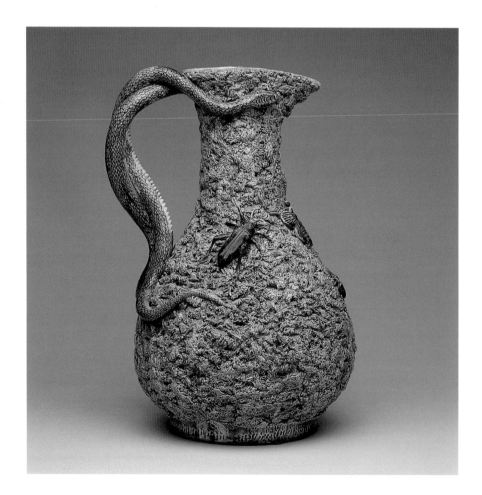

64 Plate, Manuel Mafra;
impressed "Mafra, Caldas,
Portugal" with crown;
16¼ in. (41.5 cm) diameter;
ca. 1865–87. Britannia, Grays
Antique Market, London.

65 Plate, Manuel Mafra;
impressed "Mafra, Caldas,
Portugal" with crown;
10 in. (25.5 cm) diameter;
ca. 1865–87. Britannia, Grays
Antique Market, London.

66 Pair of candlesticks,
Manuel Mafra; each
impressed "M. Mafra, Caldas,
Portugal" with crown;
each 10 in. (25.5 cm) high;
ca. 1865–87. Marty Frenkel
and Barbara Barbara
collection, Los Angeles.

67 Plate, Manuel Mafra;
impressed "M. Mafra, Caldas,
Portugal" with crown;
9½ in. (24 cm) diameter;
ca. 1865–87. Marty Frenkel
and Barbara Barbara
collection, Los Angeles.

José Alves Cunha (fl. 1860–ca. 1885)

José Alves Cunha (also known as José Alves da Cunha) established a small factory in Caldas da Rainha in 1860. He was second only to Manuel Mafra in the number of works he produced during the decades of the 1860s and 1870s.

It is likely (though undocumented) that Cunha worked for Mafra, because his work more closely resembles Mafra's than does the work of any other Caldas ceramist.[40] At its peak Cunha's factory employed ten workers, whose average daily wage was 350 reis for men and 100 reis for women. This calculates today to approximately 32 cents for men and 9 cents for women.[41] A twelve-hour workday was standard, six or seven days a week.

Cunha's work was often the equal of Mafra's. Many works by the two would be impossible to distinguish from one another were it not for their respective marks (compare, for example, nos. 82, 83, 85, and 86 to works by Mafra). Unmarked plates, especially those with common designs, are extremely difficult to ascribe.

Cunha is best known for his rendition of the famous cabbage-leaf tea service with snake handles (no. 68), taken from a late-eighteenth-century Portuguese design from the Royal Ceramics Factory in Lisbon. Mafra made a similar service (no. 26), but most of the tea services that still exist were made by Cunha, whose reputation rests largely on this specialty.

Cunha was an important Palissy follower. He used white clay from Leiria and red and white clays from Caldas, and his works were sold throughout Portugal as well as exported to England. His marks are "JAC" and "José A. Cunha" in an oval. We do not know when José Alves Cunha retired, but historical texts suggest that his sons or other relatives continued his business at least after the mid-1880s. A mark bearing the inscription "José A. Cunha Sucessor, Caldas" is dated by one source to 1895.[42]

69 Plate, José Alves Cunha; impressed "José A. Cunha, Caldas Rainha, Portugal" in an oval; 9½ in. (24 cm) diameter; ca. 1860–85. New Orleans Museum of Art: Brooke Hayward Duchin Collection (acc. no. 1997.766).

70 Pair of candlesticks, José Alves Cunha; each impressed "José A. Cunha, Caldas Rainha, Portugal" in an oval; each 8¼ in. (21 cm) high; ca. 1860–85. Cara Antiques, Newtown, Pennsylvania.

71 Plate, José Alves Cunha; impressed "José A. Cunha, Caldas Rainha, Portugal" in an oval; 17 in. (43 cm) diameter; ca. 1860–85. David Kozloff collection, Pittsburgh.

72 Mark on rear of plate in no. 71.

73 Plate, José Alves Cunha; impressed "José A. Cunha, Caldas Rainha, Portugal" in an oval; 7½ in. (19 cm) diameter; ca. 1860–85. Britannia, Grays Antique Market, London.

74 Plate, José Alves Cunha; impressed "José A. Cunha, Caldas Rainha, Portugal" in an oval; 6⅝ in. (17 cm) diameter; ca. 1860–85. Moe and Toni Wizenberg collection, Oklahoma City.

75 Ewer with lid and saucer, José Alves Cunha; each piece impressed "José A. Cunha, Caldas Rainha, Portugal" in an oval; 14½ in. (37 cm) high, 8 in. (20.5 cm) diameter; ca. 1860–85. Ricardo do Espírito Santo Silva Foundation, Duarte Pinto Coelho Collection, Museu de Artes Decorativas Portuguesas, Lisbon (inv. no. 11).

64

76 *Ewer with saucer, José Alves Cunha; each piece impressed "José A. Cunha, Caldas Rainha, Portugal" in an oval; 15 in. (38 cm) high; ca. 1860–85. Britannia, Grays Antique Market, London.*

77 *Ewer with saucer, José Alves Cunha; each piece impressed "José A. Cunha, Caldas Rainha, Portugal" in an oval; 15 in. (38 cm) high; ca. 1860–85. Britannia, Grays Antique Market, London.*

78 *Ewer with lid and saucer, José Alves Cunha; ewer and lid impressed "José A. Cunha, Caldas Rainha, Portugal" in an oval; 15 in. (38 cm) high, 8 in. (20.5 cm) diameter; ca. 1860–85. New Orleans Museum of Art: Brooke Hayward Duchin Collection (acc. no. 1997.776).*

79 Plate, José Alves Cunha;
impressed "José A. Cunha,
Caldas Rainha, Portugal" in
an oval; 9½ in. (24 cm)
diameter; ca. 1860–85.
Cara Antiques, Newtown,
Pennsylvania.

80 Plate, José Alves Cunha;
impressed "José A. Cunha,
Caldas Rainha, Portugal"
in an oval; 11 in. (28 cm)
diameter; ca. 1860–85.
Marty Frenkel and Barbara
Barbara collection, Los Angeles.

81 Plate, José Alves Cunha;
impressed "José A. Cunha,
Caldas Rainha, Portugal" in
an oval; 12¼ in. (31 cm)
diameter; ca. 1860–85.
Museu de Cerâmica, Caldas
da Rainha.

82 Plate, José Alves Cunha;
impressed "José A. Cunha,
Caldas Rainha, Portugal"
in an oval; 9¾ in. (25 cm)
diameter; ca. 1860–85.
Cara Antiques, Newtown,
Pennsylvania.

83 Plate, José Alves Cunha;
impressed "José A. Cunha,
Caldas Rainha, Portugal"
in an oval; 9½ in. (24 cm)
diameter; ca. 1860–85.
Cara Antiques, Newtown,
Pennsylvania.

84 Plate, José Alves Cunha;
impressed "José A. Cunha,
Caldas Rainha, Portugal"
in an oval; 7½ in. (19 cm)
diameter; ca. 1860–85.
New Orleans Museum
of Art: Brooke Hayward
Duchin Collection
(acc. no. 1997.774).

85 *Plate, José Alves Cunha;
impressed "José A. Cunha,
Caldas Rainha, Portugal" in
an oval; 9¼ in. (23.5 cm)
diameter; ca. 1860–85.
Cara Antiques, Newtown,
Pennsylvania.*

86 *Plate, José Alves Cunha;
impressed "José A. Cunha,
Caldas Rainha, Portugal" in
an oval; 9½ in. (24 cm)
diameter; ca. 1860–85.
New Orleans Museum
of Art: Brooke Hayward
Duchin Collection
(acc. no. 1997.777).*

69

87 Plate, José Alves Cunha;
impressed "José A. Cunha,
Caldas Rainha, Portugal" in
an oval; 9⅛ in. (23 cm)
diameter; ca. 1860–85.
Britannia, Grays Antique
Market, London.

88 Pair of vases, José Alves
Cunha; each impressed "José
A. Cunha, Caldas Rainha,
Portugal" in an oval and
incised numeral "6"; each
10¼ in. (26 cm) high,
7½ in. (19 cm) diameter;
ca. 1860–85. Museu de
Cerâmica, Caldas da Rainha.

70

91 Plate, José Alves Cunha; impressed "José A. Cunha, Caldas Rainha, Portugal" in an oval; 9½ in. (24 cm) diameter; ca. 1860–85. New Orleans Museum of Art: Brooke Hayward Duchin Collection (acc. no. 1997.779).

92 Plate, José Alves Cunha; impressed "José A. Cunha, Caldas Rainha, Portugal" in an oval and incised "No 4"; 11¼ in. (28.5 cm) diameter; ca. 1860–85. Britannia, Grays Antique Market, London.

93 *Plate, José Alves Cunha;*
impressed "José A. Cunha,
Caldas Rainha, Portugal"
in an oval; 7 in. (18 cm)
diameter; ca. 1860–85.
Cara Antiques, Newtown,
Pennsylvania.

94 *Plate, José Alves Cunha;*
impressed "José A. Cunha,
Caldas Rainha, Portugal"
in an oval; 10 in. (25.5 cm)
diameter; ca. 1860–85.
Marty Frenkel and Barbara
Barbara collection, Los Angeles.

95 *Plate, José Alves Cunha;
impressed "José A. Cunha,
Caldas Rainha, Portugal"
in an oval and incised
"No 4"; 9¾ in. (25 cm)
diameter; ca. 1860–85.
Animal Art Antiques,
New Orleans.*

96 *Plate, José Alves Cunha;
impressed "José A. Cunha,
Caldas Rainha, Portugal" in
an oval; 15 in. (38 cm) high;
ca. 1860–85. Britannia, Grays
Antique Market, London.*

74

97 Plate, José Alves Cunha;
impressed "José A. Cunha,
Caldas Rainha, Portugal" in
an oval; 9¼ in. (23.5 cm)
diameter; ca. 1860–85.
Cara Antiques, Newtown,
Pennsylvania.

98 Plate, José Alves Cunha;
impressed "José A. Cunha,
Caldas Rainha, Portugal" in
an oval and incised numeral
"6"; 6⅞ in. (17.5 cm)
diameter; ca. 1860–85.
Animal Art Antiques,
New Orleans.

José Francisco de Sousa (fl. 1860–1893)

José Francisco de Sousa, one of Portugal's more artistic makers of Palissy ware, acquired a factory in 1860 from another ceramist, António de Sousa Liso, who had founded it five years earlier.[43] Some accounts place the factory at rua do Jogo da Bola, others at rua do Conselheiro. According to industrial records of 1881, the factory employed four persons, with an average daily wage of 500 reis (45 cents). Principal clays were white from Leiria and white and red from Caldas. Records indicate that the factory was acquired in 1893 by José Augusto de Sousa (José Francisco's son) and António Moreira da Câmara. Three years later it was leased exclusively to da Câmara. After 1907 the factory was owned by José Augusto de Sousa and his brother, Salvador de Sousa.[44]

The works of José Francisco de Sousa are largely unrecognized outside Portugal because his predominant mark, "JFS" in fancy script inside an oval, is barely legible (no. 102). However, this remarkable maker deserves broader renown for his diversified color palette and artistic rendering. His works are often superior to Mafra's, and he is in our judgment among the better Caldas ceramists. The plates shown in nos. 99, 101, 103, and 105 are excellent examples of his color palette and skill. His artistic treatments are markedly more interesting than similar designs executed by Mafra or Cunha. For example, de Sousa's multiple fish on moss (no. 101) is more colorfully rendered and artistically executed than a similar Mafra plate (no. 17). We have seen no examples of works by Mafra or Cunha that compare with de Sousa's jasper fish plate (no. 99) or his lobster in basket (no. 105). De Sousa's works were sold throughout Portugal and exported to England.

99 Plate, José Francisco de Sousa; impressed "JFS" in an oval; 19⅛ in. (48.5 cm) diameter; 1860–93. Ricardo do Espírito Santo Silva Foundation, Duarte Pinto Coelho Collection, Museu de Artes Decorativas Portuguesas, Lisbon (inv. no. 141).

100 Plate, José Francisco de Sousa; impressed "JFS" in an oval; 14⅜ in. (36.5 cm) diameter; 1860–93. Ricardo do Espírito Santo Silva Foundation, Duarte Pinto Coelho Collection, Museu de Artes Decorativas Portuguesas, Lisbon (inv. no. 124).

77

101 Plate, José Francisco de Sousa; impressed "JFS" in an oval; 11 in. (28 cm) diameter; 1860–93. Marty Frenkel and Barbara Barbara collection, Los Angeles.

102 Mark on rear of plate in no. 101.

103 Plate, José Francisco de Sousa; impressed "JFS" in an oval; 14 in. (35.5 cm) diameter; 1860–93. New Orleans Museum of Art: Brooke Hayward Duchin Collection (acc. no. 1997.760).

78

104 Plate, José Francisco de Sousa; impressed "JFS" in an oval; 9⅛ in. (23 cm) diameter; 1860–93. Britannia, Grays Antique Market, London.

105 Plate, José Francisco de Sousa; impressed "JFS" in an oval; 14 in. (35.5 cm) diameter; 1860–93. Private collection.

106 Plate, José Francisco
de Sousa; impressed "JFS"
in an oval; 16½ in. (42 cm)
diameter; 1860–93.
Private collection.

107 Plate, José Francisco
de Sousa; impressed "JFS"
in an oval; 9 in. (23 cm)
diameter; 1860–93.
New Orleans Museum
of Art: Brooke Hayward
Duchin Collection
(acc. no. 1997.780).

108 Plate, attributed to José
Francisco de Sousa; unsigned;
4 in. (10 cm) diameter;
1860–93. Animal Art
Antiques, New Orleans.

81

109 Plate, José Francisco de Sousa; impressed "JFS" in an oval; 11 in. (28 cm) diameter; 1860–93. Marty Frenkel and Barbara Barbara collection, Los Angeles.

110 Plate, José Francisco de Sousa; impressed "JFS" in an oval; 8¼ in. (21 cm) diameter; 1860–93. Britannia, Grays Antique Market, London.

111 Plate, José Francisco de Sousa; impressed "JFS" in an oval; 6 in. (15 cm) diameter; 1860–93. New Orleans Museum of Art: Brooke Hayward Duchin Collection (acc. no. 1997.761).

112 Plate, José Francisco de Sousa; impressed "JFS" in an oval; 9 in. (23 cm) diameter; 1860–93. Britannia, Grays Antique Market, London.

83

113 Plate, José Francisco de Sousa; impressed "JFS" in an oval; 10¾ in. (27.5 cm) diameter; 1860–93. Britannia, Grays Antique Market, London.

114 Plate, José Francisco de Sousa; impressed "JFS" in an oval; 17 in. (43 cm) diameter; 1860–93. Britannia, Grays Antique Market, London.

Rafael Bordalo Pinheiro (1846–1905)

The most famous and successful Portuguese ceramist and Palissy follower remains virtually unknown in the United States except in knowledgeable ceramics circles. Rafael Augusto Bordalo Pinheiro was born in Lisbon into a family of distinguished artists.[45] He was one of nine children, many of whom carried on the family artistic tradition.

Manuel Maria Bordalo Pinheiro (1815–1880), Rafael's father, was a civil servant and a painter of some acclaim. His works hung in many collections, including that of Dom Fernando II, who owned five of Manuel's paintings. Manuel was a prodigious artist, producing an extraordinary number of paintings, sculptures, drawings, and engravings. His paintings, influenced by the Flemish school, were so meticulously rendered that he received commissions to reproduce the works of Diego Velázquez, Bartolomé Esteban Murillo, and several great Parisian painters. In his varied artistic career, he also designed and fabricated sets and clothing for numerous theatrical productions and illustrated literary publications.

At around the age of eleven, Rafael received his first lessons in drawing and modeling in his father's workshop; three years later he was enrolled at a nearby fine arts school, Liceu das Merceeiras. Despite his art training, Rafael displayed an interest in acting, and upon graduation he joined a local dramatics society. At first he made repairs to stage sets, but eventually he secured minor acting roles and was later accepted to the prestigious Escola Dramática.

In 1863 Rafael's father, not wanting the son to squander his arts education, secured a civil servant position for him in the Câmara dos Pares, a government agency. Probably to please his father, Rafael simultaneously attended a civil arts school, where he took varied courses, including ancient Greek and Roman architectural design. He spent his time in all but his drawing classes making caricatures or cartoons of his teachers.

While Rafael Pinheiro's father was a respected, well-established artist, many of his other children achieved similar or greater success. We have no direct evidence of their influence on Rafael, but we can assume their talents and early accomplishments played a role in his later development.

Maria Augusta Pinheiro (1841–1915), Rafael's older sister, was trained as a painter but became a nationally renowned lace designer, winning a gold medal at the Paris Exposition Universelle of 1889. She collaborated with Rafael as a ceramics painter and established her own ceramics workshop for women.

Columbano Pinheiro (1875–1929) was nearly thirty years younger than his brother Rafael. He became a noteworthy painter who exhibited in Paris and later in Lisbon. Today his works hang in the Lisbon Museu de Arte Contemporâneo, of which he was the first director.

Feliciano Bordalo Pinheiro (1847–1905), a more contemporary brother to Rafael, was a retired army colonel in 1883, when he persuaded Rafael to help him establish a ceramics factory in Caldas da Rainha. In 1884, while the new facility was being erected, Feliciano arranged for Rafael to experiment with clays and glazes at the workshop of the local Caldas ceramist Francisco Gomes de Avelar. Feliciano served as the first production manager of the Pinheiro brothers' factory until about 1892, when he retired from the business.

Two other Pinheiro brothers and a sister pursued careers outside the arts, but they still engaged in sculpture, drawing, and engraving as avocations.

In 1866, at age twenty, Rafael married Elvira Ferreira de Almeida; his dedication to drawing was so consuming that he even made sketches, watercolors, and charcoal drawings during his honeymoon. By 1870 his drawings had become full-scale political and social caricatures and were appearing in magazines and pamphlets. In 1871 and 1872 his works — in particular, two large drawings entitled *Village Wedding* and *Village Funeral*—won prizes at exhibitions in Lisbon and Madrid.

He exhibited with his father in 1868 and with his brother Columbano in 1874. At the same time, he continued drawing caricatures and cartoons, which began to receive increasing public recognition. In 1870 he launched his first publication, *O calcanhar de Aquiles* (Achilles heel), the first true political caricature pamphlet in Portugal. In 1871 and 1872 he published two additional caricature pamphlets, *Berlinda* (Game of forfeits) and *Binóculo* (Opera glasses), but sales were disappointing. The following year he traveled to England, making illustrations for several international magazines, including *Illustracion de Madrid*, *Illustracion española y americana*, and the *London Illustrated News*. His watercolors were reproduced in the *Almanac* of the *London Illustrated News*.

In 1875, after co-publishing a short-lived magazine, *Lanterna mágica*, Rafael was invited to Rio de Janeiro in August to direct a satirical magazine, *O mosquito*. One year later he moved his family to Rio de Janeiro and, having enjoyed considerable success, remained four more years, purchased the magazine, and published booklets of political caricatures. In 1879 Pinheiro returned to Lisbon and continued publishing his political cartoons and satires to a receptive public.

Throughout his life he would publish newspapers, journals, magazines, booklets, and books containing his political satires and caricatures. His last magazine, *Paróda*, was started in 1900, only five years before his death. It is evidence of Rafael's seemingly inexhaustible creative energy that he also steadily produced drawings, watercolors, and illustrations and devoted twenty-one years to ceramics.

It was his brother Feliciano's urging for partnership that drew Rafael to the full-time profession of ceramics at age thirty-seven. Feliciano had been a frequent visitor to the spa at Caldas da Rainha and an admirer of the local ceramics industry and beautiful countryside. Convinced that the pottery factories there were primitive and outmoded, Feliciano gathered a group of investors, including his friend Felisberto José da Costa, and persuaded Rafael to lend his artistic talent to a modern enterprise. In October 1883 Feliciano drew plans for the new business, to be known as Fábrica de Faianças das Caldas da Rainha. Rafael moved with his family to Caldas the next April, purchased land for the new factory, and immediately began using the de Avelar facility for experimentation and training. Rafael plunged himself into clay working and produced a small number of early pieces that today are in museums and private collections.

In September 1884 the initial phase of the new factory was completed. Rafael assumed the artistic direction while his brother managed the plant. At first the factory concentrated its production on industrial products, such as construction brick and commercial floor and wall tiles. The factory contained what was then state-of-the-art equipment, including stamping presses, glass mills, paint mills, seven tile kilns, three kilns for artistic ware, two large Minton kilns for sandstone tableware, and a calcination kiln.

By June 1885 the second phase of the factory was completed, permitting production of a full line of decorative and household tableware. The final phase, for producing large quantities of commercial tableware, was not equipped until 1888.

Rafael threw himself into his work with such passion that the factory achieved high-quality production almost from the start,[46] yet Feliciano's contributions to this success are unknown. In 1885 the company exhibited at the Portugal Commercial Exhibition in Lisbon and conducted significant business. Despite numerous orders, however, the factory was underfunded. Rafael sought government support by inviting his friend Emidio Navarro, minister of public works, to visit the facility. Navarro commissioned a public works ceramic sculpture project and proposed an annual subsidy that would begin in 1887 if the company would teach ceramic modeling, painting, glazing, and firing to students from the Industrial School of Caldas da Rainha. The contract would last for fifteen years, matriculating a maximum of 150 students per year.

For the next several years, Rafael continued to oversee the factory's artistic direction. Unfortunately, he and his brother were poor businessmen, and the enterprise, which employed more than fifty workers, continued to decline. Nevertheless, Rafael produced a prodigious number of works whose variety of colored glazes, intricate modeling, depth of color, and artistic design brought the ceramist fame. The works in which he represented crustaceans, batrachians, and other sea life were influenced by two concurrent revival movements. The more important was Palissy ware, initiated by Manuel Mafra in the 1850s, and to a lesser extent, the Manueline decorative style that dated to the early sixteenth century.

The sales of Palissy-inspired and Manueline-type ceramics, notwithstanding Rafael Pinheiro's extraordinary artistic gifts, could not generate enough revenue to overcome lagging sales of household ware and commercial tableware that were the mainstay of the business. By 1889, despite a successful commercial exhibition in Oporto that same year, the factory needed another cash infusion. The Portuguese government granted a loan that staved off impending bankruptcy and enabled the company to exhibit at the 1889 Paris Exposition Universelle. The exhibition was a great success: Rafael Pinheiro received the Legion of Honor from French president Sadi Carnot; the factory was awarded gold and silver medals; and the company received many orders, some paid in advance. Whether the orders were misplaced is not known, but none was ever delivered. Thus began a final decline in the affairs of the enterprise, which Pinheiro was never able to reorganize.

During this period Pinheiro's creative output was unabated. He created many of his greatest works, including, in 1889, a monumental eight-foot urn entitled *Jar to Beethoven* (not illustrated), which is now in the collection of the Museu de Belas Artes in Rio de Janeiro. Perhaps his most compelling work in the style of Bernard Palissy is a plate with a highly realistic depiction of fish and leaves, exquisitely rendered in complementary, contrasting colors (no. 117). It is nearly four inches in depth and employs the *verguinha* technique of ceramic basket weaving. This ceramic masterpiece, which represents the pinnacle of Pinheiro's Palissy-inspired repertoire, was produced on multiple occasions beginning in 1893. Two excellent ceramics from 1892 and 1897, both in the Palissian style, are a plate with fish (no. 115) and a plate with sea creatures (no. 116). A huge exhibition platter from 1897 depicts a still-life arrangement, in very high relief, of baskets with vegetables and sea creatures (no. 118).

By 1892, despite Rafael's efforts, the deficit of the factory in Caldas da Rainha had become so great that the original shareholders were forced to forfeit their holdings to the Bank of Portugal. Rafael, because of his years of friendship with Júlio Vilhena, the governor of the bank, was appointed director of operations, although he gradually relinquished the attendant responsibilities to others. Despite financial and organizational problems, the company continued to receive awards. In addition to the Paris medal of 1889, between 1888 and 1904 the company received gold medals from exhibitions in Oporto (1888 and 1895), Madrid (1892), Antwerp (1894), and Saint Louis, Missouri (1904).

Any discussion of Pinheiro's work must cover not only his artistry, but also the commercial side of his ceramics. The latter is not where his heart led him; in fact, this man of creativity and vision had so little interest in utilitarian ventures that it was a wonder the company survived his lack of attention to these concerns. Even so, Pinheiro enjoyed near-spectacular success with the introduction of high-relief, hand-painted, and highly glazed wall tiles. Interior and exterior home tile decoration in Portugal, which had reached its zenith around the end of the eighteenth century, revived briefly in the late nineteenth century and early twentieth.

When Pinheiro returned from the Paris Exposition of 1889, influenced by the French wave of art nouveau, he designed and executed his finest examples of relief tile art (see nos. 140 and 141), considered the best ever made in Portugal. During the next ten years, Pinheiro received numerous commissions from wealthy patrons, some of which can still be seen in Lisbon. The art nouveau influence is clear in his rendition of frogs on lily pads (no. 141) and in his crabs and eels (no. 140). Many of these tiles are still produced in Caldas da Rainha, but the reproductions lack the crisp detail and thick glaze of the originals.

Pinheiro retired to Lisbon from Caldas da Rainha in 1900, transferring total direction of the factory to his son, Manuel Gustavo Bordalo Pinheiro. Rafael continued a number of artistic activities, including the sculpting of terra-cotta busts.

Pinheiro was at least an acquaintance, if not a friend, of John Singer Sargent, the renowned English portrait painter.[47] Sargent made a pencil sketch of Pinheiro in Alcobaça, Portugal, dated 18 July 1903 and inscribed, in French: "To my excellent traveling companion and friend." We may speculate that the two were introduced by Pinheiro's younger brother, Columbano, a significant painter in his own right, but this is unsubstantiated. It is documented, however, that Sargent visited Portugal in 1903 to paint watercolors of several Portuguese towns.[48]

Pinheiro took up publishing again in 1900; he died five years later.

John Singer Sargent
(1856–1925), *Rafael
Bordalo Pinheiro*, 1903,
pencil on paper; inscribed "*à
mon excellent compagnon /
de voyage et ami / M.
Bordallo Pinheiro /
John S. Sargent / Alcobaça,
18 Juillet / 1903*"; 9½ in.
(24 cm) × 5⅛ in. (13 cm).
Dr. Martim de Albuquerque
collection, Lisbon.

89

115 Plate, Rafael Bordalo
Pinheiro; impressed "FFCR";
24¼ in. (61.5 cm) diameter;
dated 1892. Museu de
Cerâmica, Caldas da Rainha.

116 Plate, Rafael Bordalo
Pinheiro; impressed "FFCR";
11 in. (28 cm) diameter;
dated 1897. Museu Rafael
Bordalo, Câmara Municipal
de Lisboa, Lisbon.

117 Plate, Rafael Bordalo
Pinheiro; signed on front
"Caldas da Rainha /
11 Novembro 1893 / Raphael
Bordallo Pinheiro," impressed
on rear "FFCR 1895";
18¹⁵⁄₁₆ in. (48 cm) diameter;
dated 1895. Private collection.

118 *Exhibition platter, Rafael
Bordalo Pinheiro; engraved
"*RBP CALDAS*"; 47¼ in.
(120 cm) diameter; dated
1897. Museu Rafael Bordalo
Pinheiro, Câmara Municipal
de Lisboa, Lisbon.*

119 Basket, attributed to
Rafael Bordalo Pinheiro;
unmarked; 5⅜ in.
(13.5 cm) × 13¼ in.
(33.5 cm) × 8¾ in. (22
cm); ca. 1890. Museu Rafael
Bordalo Pinheiro, Câmara
Municipal de Lisboa, Lisbon.

120 Plate, Rafael Bordalo
Pinheiro; impressed "FFCR";
17½ in. (44.5 cm)
diameter; dated 1889.
Private collection.

121 Mark and date on rear of
plate in no. 120.

93

122 Jar, Rafael Bordalo
Pinheiro; impressed "FFCR";
17½ in. (44.5 cm) high,
30 in. (76 cm) diameter;
dated 1902. Museu Rafael
Bordalo Pinheiro, Câmara
Municipal de Lisboa, Lisbon.

123 Plate, Rafael Bordalo
Pinheiro; impressed "FFCR";
16½ in. (42 cm) diameter;
dated 1887. Cara Antiques,
Newtown, Pennsylvania.

124 Plate, Rafael Bordalo
Pinheiro; impressed "FFCR";
8⅜ in. (21.5 cm) diameter;
dated 1889. Animal Art
Antiques, New Orleans.

125 Plate, Rafael Bordalo
Pinheiro; impressed "FFCR";
17 in. (43 cm) diameter;
dated 1890. Museu Rafael
Bordalo Pinheiro, Câmara
Municipal de Lisboa, Lisbon.

126 Plate, attributed
to Rafael Bordalo Pinheiro;
impressed "FFCR"; 17½ in.
(44.5 cm) diameter; dated
1887 or 1897. Museu Rafael
Bordalo Pinheiro, Câmara
Municipal de Lisboa, Lisbon.

127 Wall relief, attributed
to Rafael Bordalo Pinheiro;
impressed "FFCR"; 15¾ in.
(40 cm) high; ca. 1890–
1905. Museu Rafael Bordalo
Pinheiro, Câmara Municipal
de Lisboa, Lisbon.

128 Wall relief, Rafael
Bordalo Pinheiro; impressed
"FFCR"; 17¾ in. (45 cm)
diameter; dated 1898. Museu
Rafael Bordalo Pinheiro,
Câmara Municipal de Lisboa,
Lisbon.

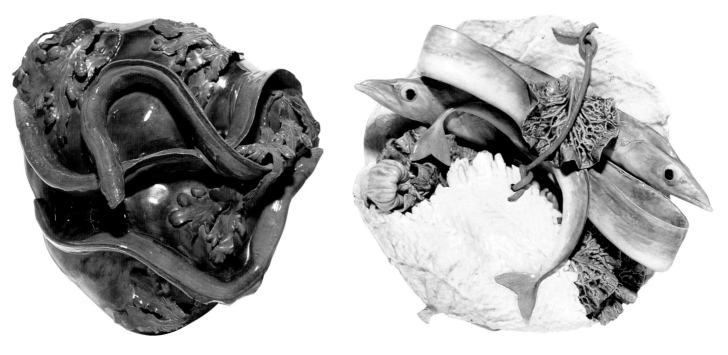

129 Pot, Rafael Bordalo Pinheiro; impressed "FFCR"; 9¼ in. (23.5 cm) high; dated 1899. Museu Rafael Bordalo Pinheiro, Câmara Municipal de Lisboa, Lisbon.

130 Plate, Rafael Bordalo Pinheiro; impressed "FFCR" and numeral "21"; 12½ in. (32 cm) diameter; dated 1888. New Orleans Museum of Art: Brooke Hayward Duchin Collection (acc. no. 1997.785).

97

131 Plate, Rafael Bordalo
Pinheiro; impressed "FFCR";
8 in. (20 cm) diameter; dated
1900. Marty Frenkel and
Barbara Barbara collection,
Los Angeles.

132 Plate, Rafael Bordalo
Pinheiro; impressed "FFCR";
11 in. (28 cm) diameter;
dated 1890. Marty Frenkel
and Barbara Barbara
collection, Los Angeles.

133 Plate, Rafael Bordalo
Pinheiro; impressed "FFCR";
16½ in. (42 cm) diameter;
1884–1905. Museu Rafael
Bordalo Pinheiro, Câmara
Municipal de Lisboa, Lisbon.

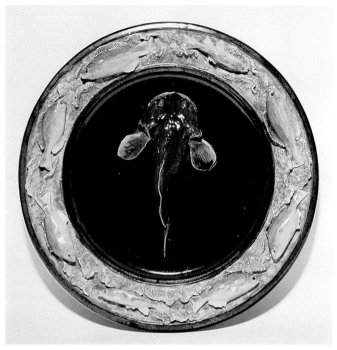

134 Plate, Rafael Bordalo
Pinheiro; impressed "FFCR";
16½ in. (42 cm) diameter;
dated 1890. Museu Rafael
Bordalo Pinheiro, Câmara
Municipal de Lisboa, Lisbon.

135 Plate, Rafael Bordalo
Pinheiro; impressed "FFCR";
16¾ in. (42.5 cm) diameter;
dated 1890. Museu Rafael
Bordalo Pinheiro, Câmara
Municipal de Lisboa, Lisbon.

136 Plate, Rafael Bordalo
Pinheiro; signed on front
"Caldas da Rainha /
Raphael Bordallo Pinheiro /
1894"; impressed on rear
"FFCR 1895"; 17¾ in.
(45 cm) diameter; dated
1895. Museu Rafael Bordalo
Pinheiro, Câmara Municipal
de Lisboa, Lisbon.

137 *Plate, Rafael Bordalo Pinheiro; impressed "FFCR"; 16½ in. (42 cm) diameter; dated 1889. Private collection.*

138 *Plate, Rafael Bordalo Pinheiro; impressed "FFCR"; 17¾ in. (45 cm) diameter; ca. 1902. Museu Rafael Bordalo Pinheiro, Câmara Municipal de Lisboa, Lisbon.*

139 Plate, Rafael Bordalo
Pinheiro; impressed "FFCR";
11 in. (28 cm) diameter;
dated 1889. Marty Frenkel
and Barbara Barbara
collection, Los Angeles.

140 Six tiles, attributed
to Rafael Bordalo Pinheiro;
unmarked; each 5¼ in.
(13.5 cm) × 5¼ in.
(13.5 cm); ca. 1890.
Museu Rafael Bordalo
Pinheiro, Câmara Municipal
de Lisboa, Lisbon.

101

141 Sixteen tiles with four
top border tiles, attributed to
Rafael Bordalo Pinheiro;
unmarked; each 5¼ in.
(13.5 cm) × 5¼ in.
(13.5 cm), border tiles
2⅝ in. (6.5 cm) × 5¼ in.
(13.5 cm); ca. 1890.
Museu Rafael Bordalo
Pinheiro, Câmara Municipal
de Lisboa, Lisbon.

102

Manuel Gustavo Bordalo Pinheiro (1867–1920)

Manuel Gustavo Bordalo Pinheiro was born in Lisbon in 1867, son of Rafael Bordalo and Elvira Pinheiro. A gifted artist, he probably moved to Caldas in the 1890s, where in 1900 he became artistic director of his father's factory. As a memorial to his father, Manuel Gustavo designed a handsome plate with a portrait relief of Rafael (no. 142).

After Rafael's death, the factory, already in precarious financial condition, was put up for auction by the Bank of Portugal. It was purchased in 1907 by new shareholders under the artistic direction of Manuel A. Godinho, but it closed in 1913. The building was eventually demolished.

In 1908 Manuel Gustavo, who was unable to secure financing for the old factory, organized a new enterprise called Fábrica de Faianças Artísticas Bordalo Pinheiro "San Rafael," which he directed until his death in 1920.[49] Many of the factory's models were designed by Manuel Pinheiro and are generally non-Palissian in subject and style. They range from classical Greek designs to sculptures of people and animals in a contemporary style. Manuel's works also include jars, urns, plates, confit dishes (no. 143), wall reliefs, and cornices, generally adorned with fruit, leaves, and animal appliqués, lizards and frogs among them. Manuel designed little in the Palissy spirit, but he continued producing Rafael Pinheiro's Palissy-inspired works (see nos. 144, 145, and 146) and thereby sustained the Palissy tradition.

In 1922 a group of Caldas businessmen bought Manuel Gustavo Bordalo Pinheiro's home and land, along with his father's and his original factory molds and casts. They erected a new factory (since rebuilt) on the site, which today employs 350 workers and exports 80 percent of its production, largely to the United States. The new company, called Faianças Artísticas Bordalo Pinheiro, produces a variety of dinner and tableware. Nearby, the home of Manuel Gustavo has been preserved as a museum, where the original works and molds of Rafael Bordalo Pinheiro are exhibited. The Rafael Bordalo Pinheiro Museum in Lisbon was dedicated to this great Portuguese ceramist's memory in 1924. A former villa, with approximately ten thousand square feet of exhibition space, it contains an extensive collection of Rafael's works, from his political cartoons and caricatures to his monumental ceramics.

142 Plate, attributed
to Manuel Gustavo Pinheiro;
unsigned; impressed on front
"Raphael Bordallo Pinheiro
1846 1905 O Mestre";
20½ in. (52 cm) diameter;
dated 1905. Private collection.

143 Confit dish, Manuel
Gustavo Pinheiro; impressed
"Bordallo Pinheiro" with frog
in a circle; 4 in. (10 cm)
high, 4¼ in. (11 cm)
diameter; 1908–20. Museu
de Cerâmica, Caldas
da Rainha.

104

144 Wall bracket, Manuel Gustavo Pinheiro (designed by Rafael Bordalo Pinheiro); impressed "Bordallo Pinheiro" with frog in a circle; 12½ in. (32 cm) high; 1908–20. Museu Rafael Bordalo Pinheiro, Câmara Municipal de Lisboa, Lisbon.

145 Vase, Manuel Gustavo Pinheiro (designed by Rafael Bordalo Pinheiro); impressed "Bordallo Pinheiro" with frog in a circle; 15¾ in. (40 cm) high; 1908–20. Museu Rafael Bordalo Pinheiro, Câmara Municipal de Lisboa, Lisbon.

146 Plate, Manuel Gustavo Pinheiro (designed by Rafael Bordalo Pinheiro); impressed "Bordallo Pinheiro, Portugal" with frog in a circle; 24 in. (61 cm) diameter; 1908–20. Museu Rafael Bordalo Pinheiro, Câmara Municipal de Lisboa, Lisbon.

Other Followers of Bernard Palissy

Many other skilled ceramists working in Caldas da Rainha in the latter nineteenth century and early twentieth century included Palissy-inspired ceramics among their repertoires.

Francisco Gomes de Avelar (fl. 1875–1897)

Nicknamed Belisário, Francisco Gomes de Avelar maintained his own factory for twenty-two years.[50] He is considered among the best Caldas ceramists for his local use of cobalt oxide to create Sèvres blue.[51] He was awarded a silver medal at the 1892 Lisbon Exhibition. Among his employees was Luísa Mafra, the half-sister of Manuel Cipriano Gomes Mafra; she taught de Avelar how to produce woven ceramic baskets. While not well known for Palissy-type ceramics, he made several such pieces, including plates (no. 151) and a tea service on a platter encircled with a snake (no. 152). He used two principal marks — entwined initials and "F. Gomes d'Avellar" — one from 1875 to 1891, the other from 1891 to 1897.

De Avelar, like Rafael Pinheiro, was a publisher, although his activities were limited to Caldas da Rainha. He founded three Caldas newspapers: *O demócrito* (1884), *O caldense* (1884–94), and *Cavacos das Caldas* (1896–97), the latter in collaboration with Pinheiro.

Avelino Soares Belo (1872–1927)

Avelino Soares Belo once worked for Rafael Bordalo Pinheiro, but in 1899 he left the Fábrica de Faianças das Caldas da Rainha to start his own enterprise, called Atelier Cerâmico.[52] The factory still exists but is now called Faianças Belo.

As a boy of eleven, Belo went to work for his father, Manuel, a fisherman, to help support the family. But the boy loved to draw and in his spare time practiced his art on paper. Dr. José Filipe Andrada Rebelo, director of the Leonor Thermal Hospital, discov-

147 *Leaf plate; impressed "José A Cunha Sucessor, Caldas" in a circle and numeral "4"; 12½ in. (32 cm) wide; ca. 1890. Britannia, Grays Antique Market, London.*

148 *Wall relief, Avelino Soares Belo; impressed "Atelier Cerâmico"; 15¾ in. (40 cm) × 11½ in. (29 cm); dated 1899. Museu de Cerâmica, Caldas da Rainha.*

149 Plate, José Augusto de Sousa and António Moreira da Câmara; impressed "de Souza filho e Câmara"; 12 in. (30.5 cm) diameter; 1893–96. Marty Frenkel and Barbara Barbara collection, Los Angeles.

150 Plate, Avelino Soares Belo; impressed "Atelier Cerâmico"; 23¼ in. (59 cm) diameter; 1899–ca. 1910. Museu de Cerâmica, Caldas da Rainha.

ered the youthful artist and showed his drawings to Rafael Pinheiro, who asked to meet Avelino. His father disapproved, and the disheartened youngster left home for a while to sell newspapers in Lisbon. He returned to Caldas when his father finally permitted him to go to work at the Pinheiro factory. By sixteen Avelino had become a skilled modeler. Later he collaborated with Francisco Elias (discussed below) on some of Pinheiro's most spectacular works.

In 1893 and 1894, Belo and Elias worked together on Pinheiro's monumental, eight-foot elaborate jar and stand entitled *Talha Manuelina*; in 1898 they sculpted the equally great *Jar to Beethoven*. In a newspaper interview that same year, Pinheiro extolled the virtues of the jar's glazer and kilnman, but he did not mention its two modelers. For reasons such as this, Belo quit the company in 1899 to found his own establishment at rua Candido dos Reis, relying not only on his skills as a modeler but on his expertise in clay, turning, painting, glazing, and firing. Once on his own, Belo produced works in the Palissian style, such as the wall relief with a crayfish (no. 148) and the plate with snakes and lizards (no. 150). He was the only Caldas ceramist to receive a medal at the 1900 Paris Exposition Universelle, though Rafael Bordalo Pinheiro and Augusto José da Cunha also submitted works.

In later years, Belo began a book on the evolution of ceramics in Caldas da Rainha and on ways to improve clay composition, colors, and glazes. Unfortunately, he commit-

151 *Plate, Francisco Gomes de Avelar; impressed "F. Gomes D'Avellar" in an oval and incised numeral "7"; 9½ in. (24 cm) diameter; 1875–97. Animal Art Antiques, New Orleans.*

ted suicide before the book was completed. His son, José Soares Belo, became manager of the factory, which remained under family management for many years.

Francisco Elias (1870–ca. 1935)

Francisco Elias began his ceramics career at sixteen as an apprentice at Pinheiro's Fábrica de Faianças das Caldas da Rainha.[53] An expert modeler, Elias was Avelino Belo's collaborator on Pinheiro's monumental works, *Talha Manuelina*, in 1893–94, and *Jar to Beethoven*, completed in 1898. He worked at the factory until it changed ownership in 1907 and then was hired by Manuel Gustavo Pinheiro at Fábrica de Faianças Artísticas Bordalo Pinheiro "San Rafael," where he stayed for eleven years. Among his specialties at San Rafael was the modeling of miniature pieces designed by Manuel Pinheiro. These were made of white clay from Leiria and took on the patina of old ivory. He did not gain public recognition until 1910, when his miniature works were exhibited by the Visconde de Sacavém in his Caldas da Rainha home.

Elias had great admiration for Rafael Pinheiro, as evidenced by the description of one writer from Caldas da Rainha: "One night when a visiting friend to Caldas da Rainha asked to see the modest monument dedicated to Rafael Bordalo Pinheiro on Copa Avenue in a desolate part of town, the only person in sight was Francisco Elias, contemplating the great ceramist's bust in awe, as if it were the first time he had seen it."[54]

In 1918 Elias left Manuel Pinheiro to concentrate on sculpting his own miniature figures, which were neither painted nor glazed. For these works he is better remembered today as a sculptor than a ceramist. Francisco Elias, as well as his brother, Herculano, included Palissy-style ceramics in their repertoires.

152 Tea service with teapot, creamer, sugar bowl, and two cups and saucers on a platter, Francisco Gomes de Avelar; each piece impressed "F. Gomes D'Avellar" in an oval; 1875–97. Museu de Cerâmica, Caldas da Rainha.

Herculano Elias (fl. ca. 1880–ca. 1908)

Herculano Elias left the employ of Manuel Mafra in 1888, taking some other staff with him, and opened a workshop at what is now rua do Jasmin in present-day Caldas.[55] There he produced works similar to Mafra's in the Palissy tradition, as in the plate with fish (no. 153). He was among the first of a dynasty that included his brothers Francisco and António and his nephews Eduardo and Júlio.

Many other ceramists in Caldas da Rainha may have contributed to the Palissy movement between 1853 and 1920, but little evidence of their production remains, save photos in catalogues or published facsimiles of their signatures or marks. The names of these artists are given here, with any known information.

João Arroja was the successor to the business of António Alves Cunha, about whom we have no information. The simplistic style of Arroja's Palissy-inspired work suggests that it might have been made between 1900 and 1920 (see nos. 154, 155, and 156).

João Coelho César (1856–1901) is recognized as among the better Caldas ceramists, and his works, some in the Palissy style, are available in the marketplace. Unfortunately, all that is known about him is that he started a small factory in 1876 and signed his works "J. C. Cezar / Caldas" in an oval.

António Moreira da Câmara practiced after 1891 and partnered with José Augusto de Sousa from 1893 to 1896. Da Câmara leased the factory alone from 1896 until 1907.

Augusto Baptista de Carvalho operated a small workshop in the early 1900s known for making souvenir ceramic pieces.

Higino de Mendonça was a ceramics painter who flourished around 1909.

Adelino Soares de Oliveira was a late-nineteenth-century ceramist who opened a ceramics factory, Fábrica de Adelino Soares de Oliveira, in Caldas da Rainha in 1892.

José Domingos de Oliveira, nicknamed Carneirinho (little lamb), founded his own workshop around 1897 after working for Francisco Gomes de Avelar.

João dos Reis made ceramic souvenirs in a small workshop located at rua do Funchal from the late nineteenth century to the early twentieth.

Etelvino dos Santos, once an employee of Rafael Bordalo Pinheiro, established her own workshop around 1904.

Eduardo S. Moreira flourished toward the end of the nineteenth century (after 1891) until early in the twentieth century.

Agostinho Noronha was a ceramics painter who worked around 1906.

Herculano Rodrigues Serra was a ceramics painter working in about 1899.

The Visconde de Sacavém operated a workshop called Oficina Cerâmica de Visconde de Sacavém first in Caldas da Rainha from 1892 to 1896, and then in Lisbon until 1899. He retired thereafter to Caldas.

Finally, Afonso Angelico, Germanol da Silva, João Duarte, N. Elias, Maria Pia, C. Sabinho, I. L. Saloio, and J. J. Saloio are identified as having made ceramics in Caldas da Rainha in the late nineteenth or early twentieth century, but no other information about them is available.

111

155 Plate, attributed to
João Arroja; unmarked;
12½ in. (32 cm) diameter;
ca. 1900–1920. Marty
Frenkel and Barbara Barbara
collection, Los Angeles.

156 Plate, João Arroja;
impressed "J. Arroja" in an
oval; 10 in. (25.5 cm)
diameter; ca. 1900–1920.
Marty Frenkel and Barbara
Barbara collection,
Los Angeles.

112

Chronology of Palissy-Style Ceramics in Caldas da Rainha (1850–1920)

1850	Manuel Cipriano Gomes (later called Manuel Cipriano Gomes Mafra) moves from Mafra to Caldas da Rainha to work in the ceramics factory of Maria dos Cacos.
1853	Manuel Cipriano Gomes acquires Maria dos Cacos's factory and produces the first examples of Portuguese Palissy ware.
1855	António de Sousa Liso opens a ceramics factory.
1860	José Alves Cunha founds a ceramics factory. José Francisco de Sousa takes over the ceramics factory of António de Sousa Liso.
1867	Manuel Gustavo Bordalo Pinheiro is born.
1884	Rafael Bordalo Pinheiro moves to Caldas da Rainha from Lisbon and opens Fábrica de Faianças das Caldas da Rainha.
1887	Manuel Cipriano Gomes Mafra retires. His son, Eduardo Augusto, takes over the family ceramics factory.
1888	Herculano Elias opens a ceramics factory.
1889	Rafael Bordalo Pinheiro wins a gold medal at the Paris Exposition Universelle. He designs and produces his first tiles.
1892	Adelino Soares de Oliveira opens a ceramics factory.
1897	The factory started by Manuel Cipriano Gomes Mafra closes.
1899	Avelino Soares Belo opens a ceramics factory.
1900	Rafael Bordalo Pinheiro retires and appoints his son, Manuel Gustavo Bordalo Pinheiro, his successor as director of the Fábrica de Faianças das Caldas da Rainha.
1905	Manuel Cipriano Gomes Mafra dies. Rafael Bordalo Pinheiro dies.
1907	Fábrica de Faianças das Caldas da Rainha is sold to new shareholders under the artistic direction of Manuel A. Godinho.
1908	Manuel Gustavo Bordalo Pinheiro organizes a new factory, Fábrica de Faianças Artísticas Bordalo Pinheiro "San Rafael."
1913	Fábrica de Faianças das Caldas da Rainha closes.
1920	Manuel Gustavo Bordalo Pinheiro dies.

Faience, Clays, and Compositions

The French word *faience* and the Portuguese word *faianças* both refer to glazed earthenware and, despite technical differences, are often used interchangeably with majolica, Palissy ware, or tinware. These ceramics are made from various clay compositions chosen for durability and are glazed with metallic oxide pigments and other ingredients. Beginning in the nineteenth century, and even to this day, flint was added to the clay mixture both to prevent cracking, shrinking, and warping and to increase whiteness and help form a secure interface between the applied surface and the body. Nineteenth-century ovens, or kilns, were generally wood-burning and very inefficient, sometimes taking as long as three days to reach sufficient temperatures. Up to one thousand pounds of wood were needed to fire ten pounds of faience. Production losses, from the cracking and breaking of 20 to 30 percent of fired works, were common, especially for large pieces.[56]

The making of Palissy ware was always a multistep process. It began with the firing of an unglazed piece, called a biscuit, which was then fired again with the glaze added. Often glazing was done in two firings. In the first, the entire biscuit would be immersed in a bath of lead glaze, or lead and tin glaze; fired; then painted with colored glazes, much as an artist would paint a canvas. For high-sheen ware, silica was added to the glaze for enameling. Once the piece was painted, it would be fired again. Occasionally, a third firing was necessary for overglazing.

Colors were made from metallic oxides: cobalt oxide produces a range of rich, jewel-like blues, depending on the concentration; copper oxide produces several colors, including reds, greens, and blues; iron oxide yields yellows and browns; manganese dioxide creates pinks and purples; and chrome oxide and antimony produce various shades of yellow.

Caldas da Rainha, with its proximity to both water from nearby rivers and clay, was perfectly situated to become a major ceramics center. The town is blessed with four major clay pits, all of them in use since the Roman occupation. Three are within a mile of the center of town, and the other, Leiria, is thirty miles north of Caldas.

Those four pits are Oiteiros, which produces a dark red clay often used by the Maria dos Cacos factory; Águas Santas, which, though the pit is now almost exhausted, still produces white clay; Gaeiras, which produces red clay; and Leiria, whose white clay is often mixed with other clays. The major clays used by the nineteenth-century Palissyists came from Leiria, Gaeiras, and Águas Santas. It was not uncommon for ceramists to use two or more clays in the same piece.

According to a former employee of today's Faianças Artísticas in Caldas, the formulas used in the nineteenth century were not recorded.[57] Production runs used different proportions, depending on the pieces to be made and on the reaction of the silica with the rest of the mixture. The following formulas are based on chemical analyses of late-nineteenth-century Caldas clay samples and of fragments from works by Rafael Bordalo Pinheiro. The analyses were conducted in 1892 by the French chemical engineer Paul Charles Lepierre.[58]

Clay sample 1	Original color:	light yellow
	Fired color:	white
MATERIAL		%
Water		9.9
Silica		63.0
Alumina		25.3
Ferric oxide		0.8
Lime		0.4
Magnesia		trace
Alkalis		0.6

This kaolin-grade clay probably came from the Águas Santas clay pit and was used for flowers and other delicate appliqués. Fired at temperatures under 1200°C, it is a soft, very pure clay, ideal for delicate modeling.

Clay sample 2	Original color:	brown
	Fired color:	white
MATERIAL		%
Water		10.5
Silica		56.2
Alumina		29.1
Ferric oxide		2.5
Lime		trace
Magnesia		trace
Alkalis		1.4

This clay probably came from the Leiria pit and was used primarily for Palissy-type works. A very plastic clay, it is ideal for small animals, especially snakes, lizards, and moths.

Clay sample 3	Original color:	light brown
MATERIAL		%
Water and volatile materials		0.6
Silica		55.2
Alumina		21.7
Ferric oxide		3.4
Lime		13.9
Magnesia		2.2
Alkalis		1.0
Unidentified		2.0

This clay sample was taken from a fragment of a pitcher by Pinheiro. This blended clay, rich in alumina, produces a very workable, hard clay providing good adhesion with the glaze. It was used for decorative tableware, such as utilitarian pitchers and vases.

Clay sample 4

Original color:	red
MATERIAL	%
Water	0.6
Silica	56.1
Alumina	21.2
Ferric oxide	4.7
Lime	12.3
Magnesia	2.1
Alkalis	3.0

This blended clay produces a result similar to sample number three, but it contains additional ferric oxide, which gives the clay a red cast.

Clay sample 5

Original color:	white
MATERIAL	%
Water	0.7
Silica	65.5
Alumina	28.3
Ferric oxide	2.6
Lime	1.1
Magnesia	0.9
Alkalis	0.8

This blended clay, taken from pieces of Pinheiro applied leaves, is similar to sample number one from the Águas Santas clay pit and was used for the same purpose.

Past and Present Price Comparisons

Collectors are often fascinated with the pricing of objects from the past, either in terms of their original cost extrapolated to present values, or in comparison with the cost of similar modern-day items. These are difficult to calculate, particularly with foreign currencies whose exchange rates are subject to revaluations and devaluations. Furthermore, contemporary versions of old pieces, if they are still made, are often of poorer quality, and their pricing may reflect factors such as inflation, use of substitute materials, and different manufacturing methods.

Rafael Bordalo Pinheiro's decorative wall tiles provide a good example. Tiles that are still produced at the Pinheiro factory in Caldas da Rainha are nearly identical to those that Pinheiro first introduced in 1889. In fact, many are cast from copies of the original molds. The frog-on-lily-pad tiles (no. 141) were offered in a 1911 catalogue from Fábrica de Faianças Artísticas Bordalo Pinheiro "San Rafael."[59] These tiles were sold four to a package for ½ escudo, equal then to 45.5¢, which, when multiplied by the average inflation factor of 13.83, equates to $6.29 per package, or $1.57 per tile.[60] Today the same tile sells in Portugal for approximately 3,000 escudos, or $17.50. We can only surmise that the staggering difference is mostly attributable to the high labor involved in making these tiles. These tiles are still hand-painted today, as they were nearly ninety years ago, when labor costs were 8¢ per hour as compared to $4.00 per hour today.

In another example, a 24-inch-diameter plate with three lobsters (no. 146) was designed by Rafael Pinheiro and offered in 1911 for 15 escudos, equal then to $13.65; multiplied by the 13.83 inflation factor, this equals $188.78. If this plate were being produced today at the Bordalo factory (it is not), it would sell for approximately $1,250 (a price based on comparable ceramics produced by the factory today). Again, the difference is likely attributable to the high labor content. However, the antique value of the 1911 example would be nearly $2,500 in Portugal and more in the United States.

A 13½-inch-high vase encircled by a lizard (similar to no. 129), designed by Manuel Gustavo Bordalo Pinheiro, was offered in 1911 for 1.2 escudos, equal then to $1.09; multiplied by the 13.83 inflation factor alone, its current price would be $15.10. However, an original vase sells for approximately $600 in Lisbon and about $900 in the United States.

A 15¾-inch-high vase decorated with high-relief frogs (no. 145), designed by Rafael Pinheiro, was offered in 1911 for 1.8 escudos, equal then to $1.64; multiplied by the 13.83 inflation factor alone, its current price would be $22.65. We have never seen one for sale, but estimate its present value in Portugal in excess of $1,000 due to the large amount of handwork.

As the reader can appreciate, it is difficult to express values from former times and in different currencies. Furthermore, high-relief ceramics in Portugal are made today very much in the same manner as they were in the past, since most of the handwork has not been automated. As a result, the inflation factor specified for "all commodities" is very likely understated.

Makers' Marks

This section contains nearly one hundred makers' marks associated with the ceramists in Caldas da Rainha during the period from 1853 to 1920, most of whom crafted at least some of their ceramics in the style of Bernard Palissy. Despite the profusion of identifying marks, there are a significant number of unmarked works in existence, many of which are difficult to attribute, principally because of a commonality of design, technique, and style among many makers. Even museum collections worldwide contain unmarked ceramics that require curatorial attributions.

Throughout history, numerous ceramics artists, workshops, and factories have neglected to identify all or a portion of their works. To this day many pieces are unmarked, though perhaps less often than in the earlier days of ceramic making. Some artisans believe that crafts, unlike art, are typically utilitarian and unworthy of signature. Some understand that their unmarked works can be mistaken for similar but more expensive items and thus bring higher prices. Some makers are uncertain about the quality of their works. Even the great Bernard Palissy failed to mark any of his works.

Portuguese ceramics that are fully marked may show not only the maker's name and mark, but the following: the maker's city or town; his or her country; the year the work was produced (either four digits or the last two digits); the worker's number or bench number (usually one or two digits or occasionally initials or a special mark); the work's model number (usually a second set of numbers); and the mark "*depositado,*" meaning registered. Works designed by Rafael Bordalo Pinheiro often show the monogrammed initials of his factory, "FFCR" (Fábrica de Faianças das Caldas da Rainha), or of the modern-day factory, "FABP" (Faianças Artísticas Bordalo Pinheiro), which still casts pieces from molds that he designed.

During the very early part of this century, Portugal adopted official changes in its spelling rules. This generates confusion when nineteenth- and twentieth-century marks and signatures are compared. For example, Rafael Bordalo Pinheiro was originally spelled Raphael Bordallo Pinheiro, which can be seen in his signature on many works. Similarly, the surname Sousa was often spelled Souza, the name Francisco Gomes de Avelar was signed by the artist Francisco Gomes d'Avellar, Avelino Soares Belo was Bello, and João Coelho César was Cézar.

In 1891 the McKinley Tariff Act required that all products imported into the United States be marked in English with the country of origin. Surprisingly, even before 1891, many Caldas potters marked their works not only "Portugal," but also "Caldas" or "Caldas da Rainha."

Afonso Angelico

João Arroja

Avelino Soares Belo

José Soares Belo

João Coelho César

António Alves Cunha

José Alves Cunha

António Moreira da Câmara

Germanol da Silva

Francisco Gomes de Avelar

Augusto Baptista de Carvalho

Higino de Mendonça

Adelino Soares de Oliveira

José Domingos de Oliveira

José Domingos de Oliveira

José Augusto de Sousa   José Augusto de Sousa and António Moreira da Câmara   José Francisco de Sousa

João dos Reis

Etelvino dos Santos ca. 1904

José Carlos dos Santos (Fábrica de Faianças das Caldas da Rainha)

João Duarte

Eduardo Elias   Francisco Elias   Herculano Elias   N. Elias

123

1907–13 (Manuel A. Godinho, managing director)

António de Sousa Liso

Eduardo Augusto Mafra

Manuel Cipriano Gomes Mafra

Manuel Cipriano Gomes Mafra

  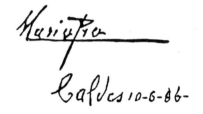

Eduardo S. Moreira

Agostinho Noronha

Maria Pia

  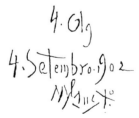

Fabrica de Faianças Artísticas Bordalo Pinheiro
"San Rafael" 1908, Manuel Gustavo Bordalo Pinheiro

(Fábrica de Faianças das Caldas da Rainha)
Tile production, 1904, Manuel Gustavo Bordalo Pinheiro

(Fábrica de Faianças das Caldas da Rainha) Regular
production, 1902, Manuel Gustavo Bordalo Pinheiro

(Fábrica de Faianças das Caldas da Rainha) Regular production
Manuel Gustavo Bordalo Pinheiro

Rafael Bordalo Pinheiro Early trials, 1884

124

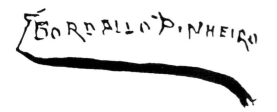
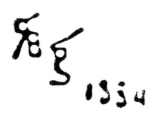

Rafael Bordalo Pinheiro early trials, 1884

Rafael Bordalo Pinheiro 1884–99

Fabrica de Faianças das Caldas da Rainha 1884–94, Rafael Bordalo Pinheiro

Ceramic tile production, 1889–1900
Rafael Bordalo Pinheiro

Ceramic tile production, 1900–1905
Rafael Bordalo Pinheiro

Common tableware production, 1888
Rafael Bordalo Pinheiro

Common tableware production, 1902
Rafael Bordalo Pinheiro

1900–1905
Rafael Bordalo Pinheiro

Construction materials, 1885–87
Rafael Bordalo Pinheiro

Special production, 1900
Rafael Bordalo Pinheiro

Large works in terra cotta
Rafael Bordalo Pinheiro

White tableware production, 1889–91
Rafael Bordalo Pinheiro

Molded production, 1898
Rafael Bordalo Pinheiro

Molded production
Rafael Bordalo Pinheiro

Rafael Bordalo Pinheiro 1884–99

Rafael Bordalo Pinheiro 1894

Rafael Bordalo Pinheiro 1900

C. Sabinho 1908

I. L. Saloio

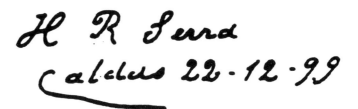

J. J. Saloio

Herculano Rodrigues Serra 1899

Visconde de Sacavém 1892–96

Unidentified Caldas da Rainha marks

Unidentified Caldas da Rainha marks

Additional markings found on many pieces, including the full date or year, worker or bench number, and occasionally the model number.

Glossary

art nouveau A style of decoration that some historians credit to French glassmaker Émile Gallé (1846–1904); it was introduced at the 1889 Paris Exposition Universelle. It is expressed mainly as floral motifs with elaborately twining tendrils (although Pinheiro also adapted the style to animal designs).

azulejo This term is both Spanish and Portuguese for tile and is thought to derive from tile decorations that were often blue (*azul*).

baroque A style of art that emerged shortly before 1600; its principal exponent was Gian Lorenzo Bernini (1598–1680). It remained current in Europe until the rise of the rococo style around 1730. A development of the Renaissance style, the baroque is characterized by lively, curved, exuberant forms; by vigorous movement in figures; and by classically derived, symmetrical ornament, which gave way to rococo's asymmetry.

biscuit Unglazed porcelain or earthenware that has been fired only once. Such ware is sometimes erroneously termed "bisque" in England and the United States. Wares deliberately left unglazed include porcelain introduced in the 1750s at the Sèvres factory in France for modeling figures and groups, perhaps because it resembled marble. Biscuit was later made elsewhere on the Continent and at the Derby factory in England about 1770.

biscuit firing A preliminary firing of unglazed pottery and porcelain that transforms the ware into the biscuit state. This is followed by glazing and decoration, unless the ware is intended to be left unglazed.

calcareous Relating to chalky clay that contains calcium carbonate.

calcine (1) The product created by exposing animal bones or hard stones, such as flint, to intense heat, thereby reducing them to a state in which they can easily be crushed for mixing in powder form with clay. (2) The combination of tin oxide and lead oxide used in the glaze of some English delftware.

clay An earth whose essential constituent is hydrous aluminum silicate. Clay in its natural state is plastic; that is, it will take and retain any reasonable shape imposed on it. It remains plastic while mixed with water, but when the water evaporates this property disappears, to return when water is again added. When exposed to temperatures above 450°C, clay becomes permanently hard. Many types and colors of clay are used, and sometimes blended, in making ceramic ware. Most clay contains iron oxide as an impurity, and this causes it to exhibit colors varying from buff to red after firing; kaolin clay remains white after firing.

cobalt blue A color produced from cobalt, a mineral that is basically cobalt aluminate; it is the widely used coloring agent for blue-and-white porcelain, especially that which is painted before glazing. First used by the Persians, it was introduced into China during the Yuan dynasty (1280–1368). Although it was used in Europe as an underglaze color from the earliest beginnings of artificial (soft-paste) porcelain, its use on the true porcelain of Meissen did not occur until comparatively late, around 1725. Cobalt blue ranges from a grayish or blackish blue to a pure sapphire, the shades and purity of the color being affected by the presence of impurities in the cobalt aluminate ore.

decoration The enhancement of the basic form of a piece of ceramic ware by any of several techniques such as painting, enameling, gilding, burnishing, applying relief work, transfer printing, etc. The term "undecorated" in factory parlance refers to glazed but unpainted ware. In appropriate cases it is said to be "in the white."

delftware Tin-glazed earthenware made at Delft, Netherlands, and also in England, where the industry was introduced by immigrant Dutch potters. The latter ware is best termed English delftware to separate it from that made in Holland. The term is synonymous with maiolica, which is Italian tin-glazed earthenware, and is often used interchangeably (though technically incorrect) with faience, tinware, and majolica.

earthenware Pottery that is not vitrified and is porous unless glazed.

enamel An opaque or transparent pigment of a vitreous nature colored with metallic oxides and applied to ceramic ware as decoration over the glaze by low-temperature firing. Enamel colors often sink deeply into the glaze of artificial porcelains, but they do not penetrate the feldspathic glazes of true porcelain; rather, they remain on the surface and are readily palpable.

faience Tin-glazed earthenware, especially that made in France, Germany, and Scandinavia. The term is of French derivation and probably comes from the sixteenth-century popularity in France of ware originating in the fifteenth century at Faenza, Italy. The technique is exactly the same as that used for maiolica and delftware, the only difference being the place of origin. In Portugal, the term also refers to majolica, lead-glazed earthenware decorated with transparent metallic pigments.

firing The process of transforming a clay body into pottery or porcelain by exposing it to heat in a kiln. The necessary temperature varies according to the type of ware, usually ranging from about 800°C for earthenware to 1450°C for oriental true porcelain. According to the type of ware, there may be several firings before the manufacturing process is complete.

flint A substance consisting of small quartz crystals in conjunction with molecules of water; after being heated to about 400°C, it can be easily crumbled or powdered. It is often added to a clay mixture to increase whiteness and improve firing results.

flux A substance added to glass, glazes, or vitrifiable bodies, such as porcelain, to lower the fusion point during firing. Fluxes are commonly added to enamel colors to lower their fusion point to slightly below that of the glaze to which they are applied, although some softening of the glaze is essential to bind the enamels to it.

glaze A coating of glass applied to a porous body to seal it against the penetration of liquids. Glazes are made by fusing silica and alumina, after a flux has been added to the silica to decrease its melting point.

impressed Indented, as distinguished from incised or cut in, by means of a stamp while the clay is still soft. Many factory marks are impressed.

incised Scratched into the body or paste of a vessel with a sharp instrument, such as a metal point, either as decoration or to record a name, date, or inscription.

jasper technique A technique developed by Bernard Palissy around 1545 to imitate the surface of jasper (a type of quartz) by mingling various colored lead glazes with metallic oxides.

kaolin A white clay, first discovered by the Chinese, derived from decomposed granite rocks and formed by water acting on the feldspar in the granite. An essential ingredient for all types of porcelain.

kiln The oven used for firing all ceramic ware.

lead glaze A transparent glaze containing silica, alumina, and lead oxide, which can produce a high gloss and allow the use of transparent metallic pigments.

maiolica Tin-glazed earthenware made in Italy during the Renaissance, usually decorated with opaque coloring. The term derives its name from the Spanish island of Majorca (*maiolica* in Italian), which exported popular Hispano-Moresque ware to Italy in the fifteenth century. Maiolica is the same technique as that used for delftware or faience.

majolica Lead-glazed earthenware decorated with transparent metallic pigments, introduced in England by Minton & Company around 1851. The company coined the term "majolica," an anglicized version of *maiolica*. Often used interchangeably in France and Portugal with faience. Some majolica may also contain tin glaze.

marks Names, letters, numbers, or symbols placed over or under the glaze on ceramic ware to indicate facts relevant to their origin and to the workers engaged in their manufacture. Marks may be impressed, incised, painted, printed, molded (sometimes raised from the surface), scratched, or stenciled.

metallic oxide The oxide of a metal used as a pigment in the decoration of pottery and porcelain, either over or under the glaze. Oxides can be suspended in an oily medium for brush application, but the applied colors before firing are different from the final colors after firing.

modeling For ceramics, the act of sculpting a ceramic ware (or from which a mold can be made for reproductions).

overglaze Decoration or marking, either painted or transfer printed, on the surface of ceramic ware after it has been glazed. Overglazes are enamels that are fixed in an enameling or muffle kiln.

Palissy ware Lead-glazed ceramics originated by Bernard Palissy in sixteenth-century France. In their most popular form, they are characterized by realistically rendered sea creatures and small forest animals, such as snakes, fish, insects, and foliage, usually in a pond setting. The term "Palissy ware" is also used for similar ceramics revived during the second half of the nineteenth century, principally in France, Portugal, and England.

Saint-Porchaire ware White earthenware with inlaid decoration believed to have originated in Saint-Porchaire, France. Also called *faïence d'Oiron* or *Henri Deux faïence*. It is believed to have been made during the reign of François I and to have continued under Henri II, the period of manufacture lasting from about 1520 to about 1550. The body is fine in texture, and the thin, overlying glaze has the appearance of a varnish, giving the ware a cream color. Before firing, designs were impressed into the clay with metal stamps of the kind that bookbinders used for tooling leather. These impressed designs were filled with colored slip, especially yellow-ocher and brown. The inlaid designs were scrolls, coats of arms, and a variety of abstract motifs popular at the time, especially those used on book covers. Relief work in the form of masks and similar details was often added. Fewer than one hundred pieces survive, and nearly all of these are in public museums. Recent findings suggest Bernard Palissy may have made some Saint-Porchaire ware at his Paris workshop (1565–72).

shard (or sherd) A fragment of pottery or porcelain, often found in archaeological digs and excavations.

slip Fine clay mixed with water in a creamlike suspension used to adhere appliqués or pottery parts to a clay body. It can also be used to coat rough clay surfaces and for relief decoration.

verguinha Literally, wicker; a ceramics technique for weaving clay strips into simulated woven basket shapes.

Notes

1. Katz and Lehr, *Palissy Ware*.

2. In nineteenth-century Caldas da Rainha, a factory, or *fábrica*, would have connoted any size production facility. With the exception of the Rafael and Manuel Pinheiro facilities, the others were workshops, studios, or ateliers.

3. Majolica was formally introduced to the English public by Herbert Minton at the 1851 Great International Exhibition at the Crystal Palace in London. Three years earlier, Minton had hired as chemist and art director Joseph-Léon-François Arnoux, manager of the Arnoux family's hard-paste porcelain factory in Toulouse. It is likely Arnoux would have been familiar with the rediscovery, five years earlier, of Palissy's lost secrets of lead glazing by Avisseau in Tours. Although no historical documents support this supposition, Avisseau welcomed many visiting potters to share his discovery, and it seems reasonable that Arnoux, either directly or indirectly, would have been a recipient of this knowledge.

4. Amico, *Bernard Palissy*, 13.

5. Ibid., 16.

6. Bernard Palissy, *L'art de terre*, quoted in Morley, *Palissy the Potter*, 2: 217–18.

7. Ibid., 228.

8. Goubert, *The Course of French History*, 106.

9. Actual remnants are displayed in Paris museums, including the Louvre and the Carnavelet, and in the Musée National de Céramique in Sèvres.

10. On Saint Bartholomew's Day, 24 August 1572, in Paris, Catholics began a mass killing of Protestants, which later extended to the provinces and lasted until October. There were approximately thirteen thousand victims.

11. The principality of Sedan, located in the northern part of France, near the Belgian border, was an independent territory ruled by Robert-Henri de la Marck, duke of Bouillon; it provided refuge for those seeking to escape religious persecution.

12. The Peace of La Rochelle in 1573, one year following the Saint Bartholomew's Day Massacre, was intended to end bloodshed between Protestants and Catholics by transferring control of the town (La Rochelle) from the throne to the Protestants. Unfortunately, it did not bring lasting peace to the country.

13. Most accounts of Palissy's life support this view; however, Amico (*Bernard Palissy*, 189) asserts that this story is undocumented.

14. Coimbra, population 80,000, is located approximately two hundred miles north of Lisbon; it is one of the oldest pottery centers in Portugal and is still active in its production.

15. *Vida do Arcebispo de Braga* (1563), and in writings from King Philip II (1582). See Calado, *Faiança portuguesa*, 3.

16. Account given by the chronicler to King Philip III of Spain (1619); description in Frei Nicolau de Oliveira, *Livro das grandezas de Lisboa* (1620); and account by Severim de Faria (ca. 1625). Cited in Calado, *Faiança portuguesa*, 5.

17. King João V was a linguist, a student of mathematics and science, and a lover of music and the fine arts. He commissioned works of art and architecture on such a grand scale that he provided full employment for artists and ateliers in several countries, primarily Italy and France. Much of the work was executed in the baroque style that was then the rage in Europe.

18. Ornaments with flowing, curved lines and fanciful intertwining of leaves, scrolls, and animal forms.

19. Fernando Augusto António Kohary (1816–1885), also known as Dom Fernando II, was the German-born husband and king-consort of Queen Maria II (r. 1826–1853). Upon her premature death, the widowed regent-king ruled while raising his two children, Pedro V (r. 1853–1861) and Luis I (r. 1861–1889) until Pedro's coronation two years later. Fernando was a passionate patron of the arts, particularly painting, ceramics, and architecture; a collector and amateur ceramist; and an influential ally of Manuel Mafra.

20. Urbino was a leading Italian ceramics center for the production of maiolica during the fifteenth and sixteenth centuries. *Grottesco* refers to the grotesque, a style of decoration popular in the sixteenth century,

ranging from loosely connected motifs of humans, plants, and animals to monstrous figures intertwined in bizarre or fanciful combinations.

21. Oporto (Porto in Portuguese) has a city population of 330,000; greater Oporto, one million, is Portugal's second largest city, next to Lisbon, and is located in the northern part of the country near the Atlantic Ocean. The city is an important seaport, industrial area, and distribution center for Port wine, once Portugal's largest export.

22. Óbidos is a tiny walled town surrounding a fortress and castle dating from the Middle Ages. It is located approximately seven miles south of Caldas da Rainha.

23. Modern-day Caldas, with a population of 20,000, continues to welcome hundreds of visitors daily to the Leonor Thermal Hospital, where curative waters are known especially to soothe asthma and rheumatism, among many other debilitating ailments.

24. Taken from a translation by Eduarda Fernandes of extracts from Correia, *Cerâmica e edificação*.

25. Other potters who supplied the Leonor Thermal Hospital were Domingos Fernandes (1488), António Dias (1555), Pedro Fernandes (1577), Francisco Alvares (1598), Gaspar Fernandes (1599), Domingos Vieira (1601), the son of António Fernandes (1607), Estevão Gomes (1609), the son of António Dias (1634), Estevão Fernandes (1656), Lucas Marques, João Francisco, and João Santos (1670). This information is from a research paper, commissioned by the author, by João B. Serra, "Cerâmica das Caldas," 1997, n. 3.

26. Translation by Eduarda Fernandes of extracts from Correia, *Cerâmica e edificação*.

27. The Madre de Deus Convent, founded by Queen Leonor de Lencastre at the beginning of the sixteenth century, is now the beautiful Museu Nacional do Azulejo (National Tile Museum) in Lisbon.

28. De São Paulo, *O hospital das Caldas da Rainha até ao ano de 1656*, 1: 104–5.

29. Serra, "Cerâmica das Caldas," 3.

30. Ortigão, *Arte portuguesa*, vol. 3.

31. João B. Serra, in *Terra de águas*, n.p.

32. A thick body is one with a heavy coating of glaze. Oiteiros is the name of a red clay pit near Caldas da Rainha.

33. De Sandão, *Faiança portuguesa*, 2: 372.

34. The Manueline style originated during the reign of King Manuel I (r. 1495–1521); it derives its forms from the sea, incorporating highly elaborate decorative accents including seashells, corals, twisted fishermen's rope, anchors, navigational instruments, and fishnets. The Manueline architectural style, which is uniquely Portuguese, also influenced the fine and decorative arts.

35. There is a surprising dearth of information on the life of Manuel Cipriano Gomes Mafra, despite his prominence in the nineteenth-century Portuguese ceramics community. We may attribute much of what was published in his time to ceramics authority José Queirós (1856–1920), from his 1907 book, *Cerâmica portuguesa e outros estudos* (Portuguese ceramics and other studies). We must surmise that Queirós's friendship with the famous Rafael Bordalo Pinheiro overshadowed Mafra's accomplishments and left him a relatively forgotten man. Queirós devoted barely a page to Mafra. The best-known modern ceramics historian is Arthur de Sandão, whose two-volume *Faiança portuguesa* is the standard reference work for Portuguese ceramics. De Sandão's passages on Manuel Mafra add little to that of Queirós, so it is understandable that our knowledge remains limited. Two well-respected ceramics scholars, Rafael Salinas Calado (curator of the National Museum of Antique Art in Lisbon) and João B. Serra (a research specialist at the University of Lisbon), have in the past ten years published several studies on Caldas ceramists, including Mafra, which have increased our knowledge. The latest and perhaps most illuminating study was conducted by Manuel J. Gandra, cultural department coordinator for the municipality of Mafra, Portugal. Much of the information in this chapter is from a paper by Gandra read at a symposium in Caldas da Rainha, June 1997, which to our knowledge has not yet been published. Despite these historians' efforts, there remains much to learn about Manuel Mafra. We could not, for example, locate even a single photograph or drawing of this remarkable ceramist.

36. Previously attributed, mistakenly, to the School of Paris; see Katz and Lehr, *Palissy Ware*, 146, no. 190.

37. According to records from 1881: *O inquérito industrial de 1881* (The industrial inquiry of 1881). Serra, "Cerâmica das Caldas," 7.

38. Although Mafra pieces are rarely dated, it is likely that demand surged in the early to mid-1860s, when Dom Fernando II made Mafra a royal supplier, and continued until at least the early 1880s.

39. This organization still functions today to encourage and promote local artisans.

40. It stands to reason that Cunha would not have opened his own factory in 1860 without prior experience. Since Cunha must have trained somewhere, and his work is nearly identical to Mafra's, we conclude that he probably worked for Mafra after 1853, but possibly earlier, at the dos Cacos factory.

41. We could not locate the currency rate conversion that applied prior to 1911, but at that time it was fixed at 1.1 escudos per dollar. Reis were officially converted to escudos in that year, at the rate of 1,000 reis per escudo. The daily rate of 32 cents for men and 9 cents for women is based on the 1911 rate.

42. Isidro and Simas, *Dicionário de marcas de faiança e porcelana portuguesa* (Dictionary of Portuguese faience and porcelain marks), 85.

43. See Queirós, *Cerâmica portuguesa e outros estudos*, 144.

44. Ibid.

45. There are nearly a dozen books on Rafael Bordalo Pinheiro, which cover many specific aspects of his life. The two most comprehensive are Dias and Machado, *A cerâmica de Rafael Bordalo Pinheiro*, and Moita, *Faianças de Rafael Bordalo Pinheiro*. It is principally from these texts that we have drawn our information.

46. One may question how Pinheiro could have achieved his considerable ceramics accomplishments in such a short period. However, it is clear that he grew up in an artistic environment and would have been so inclined. He wrote in the journal *O mundo* (The world), 4 November 1903: "Many people think I started modeling clay after I was grown. They're wrong. In my father's house I practiced modeling. . . . I've always lived among artists in my family." Quoted in Dias and Rogério, *A cerâmica de Rafael Bordalo Pinheiro*, 37.

47. Born in Florence, Italy, Sargent (1856–1925) studied in both Florence and Paris, where he first gained recognition, but most of his work was done in England, where he became the most fashionable portrait painter of his day. If indeed he was a traveling companion of Pinheiro during his 1903 visit to Portugal, the two may have communicated in French, since the inscription on Sargent's drawing of Pinheiro is in that language. Well-educated Portuguese in the nineteenth century, of whom Pinheiro was one, often spoke French as a second language.

48. Detailed in a letter to the author from Frederick J. Elsea III, 1997.

49. Dias and Machado, *A cerâmica de Rafael Bordalo Pinheiro*, 199.

50. Information on Francisco Gomes de Avelar is from ibid., 188–90.

51. Sèvres blue, or royal blue, was used extensively during the nineteenth century at the ceramics manufactory in Sèvres, outside Paris.

52. Information on Avelino Soares Belo is from Dias and Machado, *A cerâmica de Rafael Bordalo Pinheiro*, 204–9.

53. Information on Francisco Elias is from ibid., 200–203.

54. From a volume attributed to Alfredo Cunha (possibly a relative of José Alves Cunha); quoted in ibid., 200.

55. Information about Herculano Elias is from ibid., 203.

56. Katz and Lehr, *Palissy Ware*, n. 33.

57. This information is from written communication to the author from Eduarda Fernandes, 1997.

58. Paul Charles Lepierre, born in Paris, 1867, was a chemical engineer employed by the Lisbon Industrial Institute. He wrote several papers on Portuguese waters, including those of Caldas da Rainha. In 1892 Edouard Garnier, director of the Sèvres Museum, commissioned Lepierre to study Portuguese ceramics and clay. Lepierre visited nearly every ceramics factory in the country during his research. The clay compositions cited are contained in Lepierre's 1899 *Chemical and Technological Study about Portuguese Modern Ceramics*. We are indebted to João B. Serra, *Cerâmica e ceramistas caldenses*, for this information.

59. A copy of this catalogue was kindly given to me by Joaquim José Alves Saloio, a Caldas collector of Pinheiro ceramics and memorabilia.

60. The inflation factor of 13.83 is derived from Derks, *The Value of a Dollar, 1860–1989*, with extrapolations by this author through 1996. The calculations were reviewed by an economist, who concurred with their results.

Bibliography

Amico, Leonard N. *Bernard Palissy: In Search of Earthly Paradise*. Paris: Flammarion, 1996.

Bidwell, R. L. *Currency Conversion Tables: A Hundred Years of Change*. London: Rex Collings, 1970.

Birmingham, David. *A Concise History of Portugal*. Cambridge: Cambridge University Press, 1996.

Cabral, A. Lucas. *Cerâmicas de colecção A. Lucas Cabral: Catálogo geral*. Caldas da Rainha: Museu de Cerâmica, 1986.

Calado, Rafael Salinas. *Catálogo da Expo Caldas '77*. Caldas da Rainha: Museu José Malhoa, 1977.

———. *Faiança portuguesa*. Lisbon: Correios de Portugal, 1992.

Catálogo geral da Fábrica de Faianças Artísticas Bordalo Pinheiro "San Rafael." Caldas da Rainha: Fábrica de Faianças Artísticas Bordalo Pinheiro "San Rafael," 1911.

Correia, Fernando. *Cerâmica e edificação: Louça das Caldas*. Lisbon, 1935.

Cunningham, Helen. *Majolica Figurines*. Atglen, Pa.: Schiffer Publishing, 1997.

Derks, Scott, ed. *The Value of a Dollar, 1860–1989*. Detroit: Manly, 1994.

de Sandão, Arthur. *Faiança portuguesa: Séculos XVIII – XIX*. Vol. 2. Barcelos, Portugal: Editora do Minho, 1985.

de São Paulo, Jorge. *O hospital das Caldas da Rainha até ao ano de 1656*. Lisbon: Science Academy Edition, 1967.

de Vasconcelos, Joaquim. *A Fábrica de Faianças das Caldas da Rainha*. Oporto, 1891.

Dias, Aida Sousa, and Rogério Machado. *A cerâmica de Rafael Bordalo Pinheiro*. Oporto: Lello & Irmão, 1987.

The Europa World Year Book 1997. London: Europa Publications, 1997.

Friedman, Milton. *Money Mischief*. New York: Harcourt Brace Javonovich, 1992.

Gallagher, Tom. *Portugal: A Twentieth-Century Interpretation*. Manchester, England: Manchester University Press, 1983.

Goubert, Pierre. *The Course of French History*. London and New York: Routledge, 1988.

Isidro, Sónia, and Filomena Simas. *Dicionário marcas de faiança e porcelana portuguesas*. Lisbon: Estar-Editora, 1996.

Karmason, Marilyn G., with Joan B. Stacke. *Majolica: A Complete History and Illustrated Survey*. New York: Abrams, 1989.

Katz, Marshall P. *Nineteenth-Century French Followers of Palissy*. Pittsburgh, 1994.

———. "Nineteenth-Century Portuguese Palissy Ware." *Ceramics Monthly* 44 (March 1996): 50–54.

Katz, Marshall P., and Robert Lehr. *Palissy Ware: Nineteenth-Century French Ceramists from Avisseau to Renoleau*. London: Athlone Press, 1996.

Levenson, Jay A. *The Age of the Baroque in Portugal*. New Haven: Yale University Press, 1993.

Marques, A. H. de Oliveira. *History of Portugal*. Vol. 2. New York: Columbia University Press, 1972.

Moita, Irisalva. *Faianças de Rafael Bordalo Pinheiro: Exposição comemorativa do centenário do fundação da Fábrica de Faianças das Caldas da Rainha (1884–1984)*. Lisbon: Câmara Municipal de Lisboa, 1985.

———. *Guia do Museu Rafael Bordalo Pinheiro*. Lisbon: Câmara Municipal de Lisboa, n.d.

Morley, Henry. *Palissy the Potter: The Life of Bernard Palissy, of Saintes*. London: Chapman and Hall, 1852.

Ortigão, Ramalho. *A fábrica das Caldas da Rainha*. Caldas da Rainha, 1957.

———. *Arte portuguesa*. Lisbon: Clássica Editora, 1965.

Portugal: A Country Study. Vol. 2. Washington, D.C.: Federal Research Division, Library of Congress, 1994.

Queirós, José. *Cerâmica portuguesa e outros estudos*. 1907. 3d ed., Lisbon: Editorial Presenca, 1987.

Salter, Cedric. *Portugal*. New York: Hastings House, 1970.

Savage, George, and Harold Newman. *An Illustrated Dictionary of Ceramics*. London: Thames and Hudson, 1992.

Serra, João B. "Arte e indústria na transição para o século XX: a fábrica dos Bordalos." *Análise social*. Lisbon: Universidade de Lisboa, 1988.

———. *Arte e indústria na cerâmica caldense (1853–1977)*. Caldas da Rainha: Património Histórico, Grupo de Estudos da Casa da Cultura das Caldas da Rainha, 1991.

———. *Cerâmica e ceramistas caldenses da segunda metade do século XIX*. Caldas da Rainha: Centro Protocolar de Formação Profissional, 1987.

———. *Rafael Bordalo Pinheiro ontem e hoje*. Lisbon: Palácio do Beau Séjour, 1993.

———. *Terra de águas: História e cultura*. Caldas da Rainha: Câmara Municipal, 1993.

———. "Cerâmica das Caldas." Lisbon, 1997.

Weatherford, Jack. *The History of Money*. New York: Crown, 1997.

Wisely, William. *A Tool of Power: The Political History of Money*. New York: John Wiley and Sons, 1977.

Index